Library Skills

Guide

Revised 2019

Homeschoolers of Maine
P.O. Box 159, Camden, ME 04843
Telephone: 207.763.2880   Email: homeschl@midcoast.com
www.homeschoolersofmaine.org

Table of Contents

NOTES:

INTRODUCTION

Thank you for supporting Homeschoolers of Maine by choosing one of our carefully constructed unit studies for your student.

In each unit study, HOME strives to provide at least one question or activity within each of the required subject areas: Math, Language Arts, Social Studies, Science, Health, Physical Education, Maine Studies, Computer, Library Skills, and Fine Arts. Bible is also included, and occasionally Foreign Language, for those who would like to cover those additional areas. This helps to illustrate how a study on a single subject can cover multiple required areas.

This study is not a conclusive study of the subject, but is intended to spark the student's interest by asking them questions and providing them with basic direction in which to begin pursuing their study of the subject. In most cases, it does not contain answers to the questions asked. This is intentional. Our unit studies are designed to help students explore, discover and develop their own perspective on various subjects that are of interest to them.

Students should in no way be confined to the questions and activities contained here. If their level of interest widens or veers off in another direction, encourage them to follow their passion.

Teaching library skills is required by Maine state law for homeschoolers. This guide will give you some simple assignments and a basic introduction to the library and its resources. It is designed to be flexible. You can use it, completing the whole packet in one year. Or you can work your way through it over the course of several years, depending on the student's age, ability and interest level.

At the end of each section is a space to put the date that the individual section was completed for record keeping purposes.

This is designed to be a basic guide and not a comprehensive study in library skills. Please see it as a springboard to get you started, but do not be limited by its content. At any and all points, feel free to dig deeper and go further than what is here.

The back side of each page has been left blank, to allow for additional space for student writing, drawing, or parent notes. It also makes it easier if you choose to remove pages for your year end assessment portfolios.

NOTES:

Before You Begin

Sometimes it can be challenging to figure out how to show progress when a student is working on a unit study. Before you begin this study, ask the student to give you a brief narrative of what they already know about the subject of this HOME unit study. Write this out for younger students, have older students write it out for themselves, here. When you finish the study, there is a page at the end entitled, *What I Learned,* for students to write down new things that they learned during the study. The comparison of these two pages can be used for portfolio reviews to document that progress in learning was made by the student.

_____

_____

_____

_____

_____

_____

_____

_____

_____

_____

_____

_____

_____

_____

_____

_____

_____

_____

_____

_____

_____

_____

_____

_____

_____

_____

_____

_____

_____

Date Begun: _____

NOTES:

YOUR LOCAL LIBRARY

Do you know where your local library is? _____

Have you visited it? _____

Are there other libraries in your town that you have access to?

_____
_____
_____

Do you or someone in your family have a library card? _____

Visit your local library. If you don't have a library card, ask what you need to do to get one. You will need one as you progress through this guide.

What is the name of your head librarian? _____
What is the head librarian's job? _____

What is the name of your children's librarian? _____
What is the children's librarian's job? _____

Draw a map of your library.

Be sure to find and label the following areas:

Children's Area
Circulation Desk (where you check out books)
Book Drop
Computer Stations
Exits
Restrooms
Any other area that is important to you and your family

Request a copy of your library's rules/lending policies. Read them together as a family.

How long can books be checked out for? _____

NOTES:

Can they be renewed? _____ How many times? _____

What other materials are available at your library?

_____

_____

_____

How long can these materials be checked out for?

_____

_____

_____

Can you borrow materials through your library from other libraries? _____

Date Completed: _____

NOTES:

ALL ABOUT BOOKS

Vocabulary – Define the following words that have to do with books:

Atlas: _____

Audio Book: _____

Author: _____

Bar Code: _____

Call Number: _____

Chapter: _____

Copyright: _____

Dedication: _____

Dictionary: _____

Encyclopedia: _____

Epilogue: _____

Fiction: _____

Glossary: _____

Hard Cover: _____

Illustrator: _____

Index: _____

Introduction: _____

Large Print: _____

Non-fiction: _____

Picture Book: _____

Preface: _____

Publisher: _____

Spine: _____

Table of Contents: _____

Thesaurus: _____

Title: _____

Types of Books – There are many different kinds of books. Below is a list of some of them. Put checks beside the ones you have at home or the ones your library has.

_____ Picture Books   _____ Non-fiction

_____ Picture Story Books   _____ Biography

_____ Folk Tales   _____ Poetry

_____ Fairy Tales

_____ Legends

_____ Historical Fiction

_____ Realistic Fiction

_____ Science Fiction

_____ Modern Fantasy

NOTES:

Book Awards – Books often receive awards. Look up each of the following awards. What is it for? List five books that have received the award.   Indicate any books you've read that have received any of these awards.

Chickadee Book Award: _____

_____

_____

_____

_____

_____

Caldecott Award: _____

_____

_____

_____

_____

_____

Maine Student Book Award: _____

_____

_____

_____

_____

_____

What other medals are there for books? Have you read any books that have received these medals?

_____

_____

_____

_____

_____

Date Completed: _____

NOTES:

ALPHABETIZING

Fictional books are generally organized by the last name of the author. Number each of the following authors to indicate the order they would be arranged in. When two authors have the same last name, then the first name is used.

_____ J.R.R. Tolkien

_____ Stephen King

_____ Judy Blume

_____ A. A. Milne

_____ Rick Riordan

_____ Mary Pope Osbourne

_____ Cynthia Lord

_____ Gary Paulson

_____ Holly Black

_____ Max Brooks

_____ Laura Ingles Wilder

_____ Beatrix Potter

_____ Mark Twain

_____ Jane Austen

_____ Charles Dickens

_____ Charlotte Bronte

_____ Emily Bronte

_____ Louisa May Alcott

_____ Susan Collins

_____ Chris D'Lacey

_____ C.S. Lewis

_____ Eoin Colfer

_____ Tony DiTerlizzi

_____ Douglas Adams

Date Completed: _____

NOTES:

WHAT SYSTEM?

There are two different systems used to organize non-fiction books in the library. One is the Dewey Decimal System. The other is the Library of Congress System.

Do you know which system your library uses? _____

Knowing these systems will help you be able to more easily locate non-fiction books.

Who is Melvin Dewey? _____
For what purpose did he develop the Dewey Decimal System? _____
_____
_____
_____
_____

Match the following number groups with the appropriate subject breakdowns:

000	Philosophy & Psychology
100	Language
200	Computers
300	History & Geography
400	Technology
500	Religion
600	Computer Science, Information & General Works
700	Literature
800	Social Science
900	Arts & Recreation

NOTES:

Who designed the Library of Congress system? _____

For what purpose was it designed? _____

_____

_____

_____

Other than the Library of Congress, do you know of another local library that uses this system of organization? _____

Match the letters with the appropriate subject section.

A	Bibliography, Library Science
B	Agriculture
C	Naval Science
D	General Works
E	Auxiliary Science of History
F	Military Science
G	Philosophy, Psychology & Religion
H	Technology
J	World History (except American)
K	Social Science
L	American History
M	Education
N	Local History of US, British, Dutch, French & Latin America
P	Language & Literature
Q	Music
R	Law
S	Political Science
T	Medicine
U	Agriculture
V	Fine Arts
Z	Geography, Anthropology & Recreation

Date Completed: _____

NOTES:

USING THE CARD CATALOG

Often times we learn to use the card catalog before we really understand the system that is behind it. You may already be familiar with your library card catalog, but now you know why it works the way it does.

Use the card catalog to locate the following books in your library. If your library doesn't have them, just make a note to that effect.

Search by Title:

_____ Little House on the Prairie

_____ My Side of the Mountain

_____ Newcomb's Wildflower Guide

Search by Author (list one book by the author):

_____ Laura Ingalls Wilder _____

_____ A.A. Milne _____

_____ Dr. Seuss _____

Search by Subject (list the call number of one book):

_____ wildflowers _____

_____ mammals _____

_____ Italy _____

Search by Key Words (list one book containing the key word):

_____ Maine mountain _____

_____ cat care _____

_____ pinecones _____

Date Completed: _____

NOTES:

MINERVA? URSUS?

Depending on your library, you'll discover it is a part of one of these larger groups. What are they? Are they important to your use of the library and its resources? Do a quick online check and see what you can learn about each one and the libraries that are involved.

MINERVA:

_____
_____
_____
_____
_____

URSUS:

_____
_____
_____
_____
_____

Which system does your library use?

_____

Date Completed: _____

NOTES:

ONLINE LIBRARY RESOURCES

MARVEL! – An online, virtual library, it's not just for the kids. This is a great resource for homeschooling parents as well. Visit MARVEL! at http://libraries.maine.edu/mainedatabases/ and learn more.

_____

_____

_____

Mango Languages – Some libraries around the state offer Mango Languages on their website. Here is a way to learn a foreign language from home. See if your library, or one you can easily access, has this program available.

_____

_____

_____

LearningExpress – LearningExpress helps students and adult learners improve the skills required for academic and career success. The LearningExpress Library™ platform provides a comprehensive selection of educational resources for basic skills mastery, academic success, job preparation, and career advancement. Also included in this great resource are popular software tutorials, Internet instruction and basic computer instruction.

_____

_____

_____

_____

_____

Check with your librarian to see what services your library offers to folks online. List them here:

_____

_____

_____

_____

_____

Date Completed: _____

NOTES:

BOOKS BY MAIL

Many small towns and outlying areas of Maine do not have access to full service libraries. For those who do not, the Maine State Library offers a program called Books by Mail. Learn more about this program and whether or not you qualify, based on where you live, at
http://www.maine.gov/msl/outreach/booksbymail/

_____

_____

_____

_____

_____

Date Completed: _____

NOTES:

GENEALOGY

What does genealogy have to do with library skills? The local library is often a great resource for those doing genealogical research. Genealogy is a great way for homeschoolers to teach and learn history about their family, their heritage and their local area. The state library has a whole page on their website dedicated to genealogical research. Many local libraries have rooms, or at least sections of their library dedicated for this.

Visit http://www.maine.gov/msl/services/genealogy/ to learn more about what the Maine State Library offers.

_____
_____
_____
_____
_____

Ask at your local library what resources they have available to those interested in doing genealogical research.

_____
_____
_____
_____
_____

Date Completed: _____

NOTES:

FINAL PROJECT

Choose one book to read. Share the information required to locate the book in your library.

Title: _____

Author: _____

Call #: _____

Subject: _____

Illustrator: _____

Publisher: _____

Copyright Date: _____

Number of Pages: _____

Something about the book that would inspire someone else to want to read it:

_____

_____

_____

_____

_____

Date Completed: _____

NOTES:

What I Learned

In this section, ask the student to narrate what they learned that they didn't know when they began this study. What new discovery did they make during the study? What did they enjoy most? What do they know now that they didn't know before? These are all good questions to ask, if the student needs prompting.

_____
_____
_____
_____
_____
_____
_____
_____
_____
_____
_____
_____
_____
_____
_____
_____
_____
_____
_____
_____
_____
_____
_____
_____
_____
_____
_____

Date Completed: _____

NOTES:

NOTES:

Made in the USA
Middletown, DE
12 September 2019

Now that you understand the importance of consuming regular meals and snacks, you may have questions about how to begin to make these recommended changes. Taking steps will be particularly difficult if you've had an eating problem for a long time. For example, it may be overwhelming to consider eating three regular meals and two snacks a day when you've gone for years without either breakfast or lunch. Remember that this prescription represents the *ideal*. Your therapist will modify the prescription so that it is appropriate and realistic for you. For example, if your pattern has been to eat in a completely chaotic fashion, your therapist may start off by having you reinstate only one of the three daily meals and one of the two scheduled snacks. Your therapist understands that change is hard. He or she will encourage you throughout the program to take small steps when making behavioral changes. This means giving yourself permission to proceed at a pace that is comfortable for you. Talk with your therapist about any concerns relating to pressures to make changes that seem too drastic. Like other individuals with eating disorders, you may pressure yourself to "do a perfect job" in any challenge you take on, including the way you do therapy, and your process of recovering from your eating disorder. We support movement forward, but we shun perfectionism—that kind of approach merely replaces one set of problems with another.

Another frequently expressed concern is the initial perception that you "can't do" the treatment at all. Fear of failure seems to be typical for individuals with eating disorders, who may learn to avoid situations in which success is not guaranteed. We believe that you can do it, in spite of your fears and the real difficulties associated with changing long-standing problem eating patterns. Think about it: you probably would not have decided to begin treatment for your problem if you weren't motivated and optimistic about your ability to change. It is important that you establish reasonable expectations. Once you feel confident that you can make the recommended changes at a comfortable pace, some of your fears about failing in treatment should disappear. Again, discuss these concerns with your therapist. Keep in mind that setbacks during treatment are expected. Consider any setbacks as learning opportunities that provide you with information about the factors that continue to adversely affect your eating. Remember: your eating disorder did not develop overnight and cannot be resolved in a few days. It is important for you to be prepared in advance for the ups and downs that come when you attempt to change, particularly as you make improvements in your eating and begin to experiment with increasingly challenging situations.

Inducing Vomiting

Another way to eliminate dietary deprivation is to discontinue all forms of purging. Self-induced vomiting provides no benefits. You need to always keep in mind that food is absorbed rapidly. Calories from ingested food are quickly absorbed, starting in the mouth and continuing as the food makes its way through the stomach to the intestines. Even if you feel you've been able to purge most of the calories you took in, this is simply not true. A sizable fraction of calories consumed in a binge is, in fact, absorbed. Self-induced vomiting is an inefficient method of ridding the body of calories. Moreover, eating followed by purging, often followed by another binge and more purging, leads the body to give false signals regarding hunger and fullness. Those who purge are receiving faulty feedback about their nutritional status from their bodies and, in the end, are likely to eat more, thus maintaining the binge-and-purge cycle.

Vomiting (and the other forms of purging) also has undesirable health consequences. Of these, the most important may be dental decay caused by the acid in your mouth combining with sugars in the binge food. In a small proportion of bulimics, the body's potassium level is depleted, negatively affecting cardiovascular function. This is called hypokalemia. In some bulimics, there is marked swelling of the salivary glands, giving an appearance of having the mumps. There are many reasons to stop purging.

Abusing Laxatives

Although it might be difficult to consider not vomiting at this early point in treatment, many patients find it relatively easy to give up other purgatives (laxatives, water pills, etc.) and go "cold turkey."

First, laxative abuse is not an effective method of ridding the body of calories. In fact, it is the least effective method of all. By the time food reaches the part of the intestinal tract that is emptied by laxatives, all the calories have been absorbed. Second, laxative use leads to cycles of dehydration and rehydration, causing water-weight gain. This leads to negative feelings about body size. Third, using stimulant laxatives reduces the normal contractions of the intestines, making it necessary for patients to continue using them to avoid constipation.

Even though there may initially be some feelings of discomfort associated with giving up laxatives, including constipation, bowel discomfort, and cramping, and temporary weight gain due to rehydration, they will dissipate over time. This will take approximately 10–14 days as your own digestive mechanisms resume their normal functioning. Keep in mind that the majority of individuals who abuse laxatives have relatively little trouble stopping. Some use simple methods of treating constipation, such as consuming additional bran, fruit, salads, and water. The best method is to stop the laxatives abruptly, throwing away all your supplies. Slowly cutting back on laxative use will simply prolong the side effects of laxative withdrawal. It may be useful to complete a cost–benefit analysis about giving up laxatives, comparing the perceived benefits with the costs to your physical health and sense of well-being. To get you started in this analysis, remember that laxatives do very little to eliminate excess calories. Although they do rid your body of fluids to the point of causing dehydration, you regain this fluid weight immediately upon drinking.

Pleasurable Alternative Activities

As described by the model of bulimia, several interrelated factors contribute to binge eating. Some of the most common triggers are hunger, negative moods, and boredom. (These and other binge triggers will be discussed in more detail in Chapter 8.) Low moods often stem from an inability to shake certain negative thoughts or perceptions. These thoughts might come from any number of sources (e.g., interpersonal interactions, feelings about eating or your body). Boredom represents one type of low mood that sets in when you have difficulty handling unstructured time. Both of these situations seem to trigger binge-eating episodes in many bulimics.

Effectively managing these risk factors involves refocusing on some alternative, distracting, and pleasurable activity that is incompatible with binge eating. Even making the effort to engage in an alternative activity tends to push the troubling thoughts and feelings into the background, allowing for a fresh and more optimistic perspective. This can be very helpful in overcoming the urge to binge. Your challenge then is to create a list of pleasurable and distracting alternative activities that can help keep you from falling victim to some of the emotional influences that make you binge.

Although it may sound simple, creating this list is quite a challenge. Commonly, bulimics report difficulty coming up with activities for this list. They acknowledge having spent an increasing amount of their time over the years involved in eating and related activities and may have a hard time getting in touch with former interests and hobbies. When asked for a list of alternatives, bulimics tend to include aversive activities, such as completing household chores like doing laundry or paying bills. Given the types of activities that tend to appear on their lists, it isn't hard to understand why binge eating seems the more desirable option!

The goal of this exercise is to compile a list of pleasurable alternative activities that can compete with your urge to binge. Physically engaging activities may work best, perhaps because, to the degree that they diffuse tension and stress, they are able to mimic the beneficial effects of binge eating and purging. Other soothing activities may involve an "indulgence" such as taking a hot bubble bath, watching a movie, or getting a massage. Again, the objective in creating this type of list is to distract yourself from the negative thoughts and emotions that might trigger an urge to binge and purge. List your alternative activities on the worksheet provided, keep it handy, and feel free to add to it at any time!

Your therapist may introduce you to a method for problem solving if you have difficulty creating your list. Problem solving is described in more detail in Chapter 10.

Pleasurable Alternative Activities

1. _____

2. _____

3. _____

4. _____

5. _____

6. _____

7. _____

8. _____

9. _____

10. _____

For the Binge-Eating Patient

Regular eating, in the form of three meals and two snacks a day, is as central to the progress of the binge eater as it is to that of the bulimic. The content of the food consumed is of greater importance for binge eaters, however. Unlike bulimics, whose weights are within the normal range, binge eaters may need to lose weight while simultaneously working on their eating-disordered behaviors. Binge eaters should decrease their fat intake to no more than 30% of total calories in addition to controlling their portion sizes. Also, regular exercise is a useful addition to the program for binge-eating patients. Taking a 30- to 45-minute walk three or more times a week will help you control your weight. It is also a pleasurable alternative activity that can compete effectively with food. Patients with binge-eating disorder demonstrate a tendency to put on weight during cognitive-behavioral therapy; hence, it is important if you are a binge eater to combine some of the elements of a weight-control program with this program. These include weekly weighing (as for bulimia nervosa), and two elements already noted: instituting a regular exercise program and cutting down on the amount of fat consumed.

Unlike the patient with bulimia nervosa, most patients with binge-eating disorder do not exercise regularly, if they exercise at all. The first step is to record the frequency and duration of any form of physical movement, including incidental exercise (e.g., taking the stairs instead of the escalator) and intentional, planned exercise in Column 5 of your Daily Food Record. The most promising and least costly exercise program is taking a brisk walk of at least 30–45 minutes a day three to four days each week. If you have never engaged in regular exercise, develop a graduated schedule of physical activity. For example, start by walking for 10 minutes at a moderate pace four times a week. Or, start with 30 minutes of moderately paced walking once or twice a week. Make sure that the exercise is as enjoyable as possible. Wear comfortable shoes and walk at a time that will fit most easily into your schedule. The decisions you make to allow exercise to be easy and enjoyable are extremely important in that they set the stage for your maintaining an exercise regimen over the long term. For example, if you are not a morning person, making a firm decision to start walking at 6 A.M. is not likely to hold. On the other hand, even if you realistically plan to start walking after you complete your workday, it is still important to prepare in advance. Will you bring your exercise clothing to work, or will you change once you get home? If you plan to change at home, how will you motivate yourself and resist the urge to hit the refrigerator or sit in front of the TV or use the telephone or computer? If you have other exercise equipment, such as a stationary bicycle, treadmill, or elliptical machine, you can use it instead of walking. Remember, thoughtful planning to create optimal and "easy" exercise situations will always apply. The goal is to develop a convenient and pleasurable exercise program that you can keep up with. If you have already begun a regular exercise regimen, discuss this with your therapist, who will help you adjust the level of exercise depending on your responses to your program over time.

Summary

In this chapter, we discussed the model of bulimia and binge-eating disorder. The model draws links between dietary restriction (or purging), binge eating, and low mood states, and dictates the interventions presented in this program, including an initial prescription of regular meals and snacks eaten by the clock. We underscored the importance of participating in pleasant alternative activities incompatible with eating and taking control over any stimuli or "inappropriate" situations that have become associated with eating. Finally, we discussed some common reactions to recommendations for change, such as perfectionist expectations and fears of failure. More than anything, we want you to experience the treatment as an opportunity to learn more about your eating problems and to risk making the kinds of changes that, while scary and difficult, are guaranteed to lead to your eventual success in overcoming your eating disorder. We are tremendously hopeful that our program can help you, and we wish you much luck in getting started. Please review the material presented in this chapter before going on to the next.

Homework

✎ Continue self-monitoring by keeping Daily Food Records.

✎ Review the cognitive-behavioral model of bulimia and binge-eating disorder as it applies to you.

✎ Begin to regularize your eating by consuming three meals and two snacks per day.

✎ For binge eaters: Decrease your daily fat intake.

✎ Develop a list of Pleasurable Alternative Activities and participate in at least one during the week.

✎ For binge eaters: Develop an exercise program and incorporate it into your routine. Record your exercise sessions on the Daily Food Record.

Self-Assessment

Take some time to review the contents of this chapter and complete the following self-assessment. Answer by filling in the correct words or phrases. Answers can be found in the Appendix.

1. Name the factors included in the model of binge eating and briefly describe the interrelationships among these factors.

   _____

   _____

   _____

   _____

2. Based on the model, which is the first step you must take toward interrupting the cycle?

   _____

   _____

   _____

   _____

3. Name the various types of dietary restriction.

   _____

   _____

   _____

   _____

4. Is weight gain a necessary consequence of normalizing your meal pattern? Explain.

   _____

   _____

   _____

   _____

5. For what reasons might pleasurable alternative activities help
    you prevent binge episodes?

    _____

    _____

    _____

    _____

Chapter 5

Medical Consequences of Bulimia Nervosa and Binge-Eating Disorder

Goals

■ To learn about alternative forms of purging and the medical complications of your eating disorder

Review of Previous Chapter

The last chapter presented a model showing the interrelationship of certain factors that contribute to the cycle of binge eating. By reading, reviewing, and rewording the model to fit your own experiences, you will better understand the factors that maintain your eating disorder. Based on your understanding of the model and the data from your Daily Food Records over the past week, you should have begun the process of correcting your problematic eating behaviors. We hope you have been working toward a regular pattern of eating and have started participating in pleasurable alternative activities that are incompatible with eating. You should also be weighing yourself weekly. If you are bulimic, you should be decreasing the frequency of your purging episodes too. Make sure to use the comments column of your Daily Food Record to identify the situational factors related to any particular episode of eating.

Overview

This chapter will provide information about alternative forms of purging and the medical complications of bulimia nervosa and binge-eating disorder.

Laxatives

Perhaps, like many patients with bulimia nervosa, you use laxatives in addition to self-induced vomiting as a form of purging. Or maybe you use only laxatives to purge, relying on large quantities of laxatives that stimulate the bowel—much larger than the amount suggested for regular use—following a binge. However, the bowel adapts to the use of such laxatives, and constipation follows, thus maintaining the laxative habit. The chronic use of laxatives can lead you to become dehydrated and will deplete your body's stores of potassium. Also, laxatives are an ineffective method of ridding the body of calories. Experience suggests that the most effective method of dealing with laxative abuse is to stop their use abruptly, that is, go "cold turkey," as described in Chapter 4.

Although you may experience side effects associated with stopping, for example, constipation, bloating, and/or abdominal discomfort, these effects are relatively short-lived, lasting only about 10 days in most cases. Sometimes a prescription for bulking agents (that are laxative-like in their effects but more mildly so), such as Metamucil, or a diet high in fiber, may help return the bowel to normal function.

Diuretics

Less commonly, patients with bulimia nervosa abuse diuretics or water pills to decrease feelings of bloating and mistakenly believe they can better maintain their weight and shape this way. Chronic use of diuretics leads to kidney (renal) damage and even renal failure, which requires dialysis. It is important for you to let your therapist know if you have used diuretics in large doses. If so, you will need a complete medical evaluation to determine your level of kidney functioning. Experience again suggests that abruptly stopping the diuretic is the best approach. When you discontinue the use of water pills, expect to retain some water and possibly experience bloating and the swelling of some body parts.

Ipecac

Occasionally, patients who have difficulty inducing vomiting use ipecac, a medication that causes nausea and vomiting. Chronic use of ipecac is dangerous and may lead to cardiomyopathy (deterioration of the cardiac muscle) and heart failure. Because of this potential complication, we advise anyone using ipecac to stop immediately.

Medical Complications of Bulimia Nervosa

Detailed medical investigations of patients with bulimia nervosa reveal only a few typical problems. The most common issues are dental and periodontal problems. Because of the sugars consumed and the acid in the mouth that accumulates with vomiting, severe erosion of dental enamel may occur. In many cases, metal fillings can be seen protruding from the tooth because the enamel around the filling has been eroded. Multiple dental caries, tooth decay caused by an infectious disease that damages tooth structures, are often found. Periodontal or gum infections may also occur. In severe cases, the bone surrounding the teeth becomes eroded. We recommend that all patients with bulimia nervosa who are not seeing a dentist regularly begin to do so.

The next most frequent problem is swelling of the salivary glands, which makes it look as though you have the mumps. Such swelling is temporary and requires no treatment. About 5% of patients with bulimia nervosa are found to have a low level of potassium, also called hypokalemia. Although only 1 in 20 bulimics has a lowered level of potassium in their blood, we recommend that all bulimics have their blood electrolytes checked. Hypokalemia may be associated with marked feelings of weakness, difficulty concentrating, and fainting. Low levels of potassium are associated with changes in the electrocardiogram and may lead to fatal cardiac arrhythmia. The risk of heart attack is particularly high for anorexic and low-weight bulimic patients. Your physician can prescribe a simple potassium supplement that will alleviate the problem.

The malnutrition associated with bulimia nervosa, including depletion of fat, is often associated with undue sensitivity to cold, dryness and coarsening of the skin, and hair loss. Also, osteoporosis may occur, occasionally leading to fractures, especially in bulimics who engage in heavy exercise. Rare complications include spitting up blood from small tears in the esophagus that result from purging. Cases of ruptured stomachs have also been reported following very large binges. Foreign objects may also occasionally be swallowed in the course of a binge. For example, one of our patients swallowed a spoon in a particularly voracious eating episode, necessitating its surgical removal.

Medical Complications of Binge-Eating Disorder

Patients with binge-eating disorder tend to steadily gain weight. It has been shown that individuals with higher levels of body fat are more likely to have the disorder. In most clinical samples of individuals who are overweight, between one quarter and one third will meet the criteria for binge-eating disorder. Therefore, the medical complications associated with this disorder are the same as those for people who are overweight or obese. Among the conditions frequently seen in such patients are high blood pressure, diabetes, and high levels of fat in the blood. Other complications include osteoarthritis, gall bladder disease, and menstrual disturbances. Finally, it should be remembered that in addition to the guilt that individuals with binge-eating behavior feel about their disorder, they often encounter social rejection because of their overweight, which can lead to low self-esteem.

Issues Regarding Weight

Patients with bulimia nervosa vary considerably in their weights, ranging from near anorexic to obese. Individuals with a body mass index (BMI) of less than 18.5 are considered underweight. The body mass index is a measure of body fat based on height and weight that applies to both adult men and women. A BMI of 30 or greater indicates obesity. Since weight and shape concerns are an important part of bulimia nervosa, your feelings about your weight and shape may affect your perceptions of this treatment program.

The Underweight Patient

Apart from the potential nutritional problems previously noted, you may feel anxiety regarding the potential for weight gain once you abandon dietary restriction, purging, and excessive exercise. You may even be overly fearful of changing your eating habits during the first phase of treatment. If you are underweight, be honest with your therapist. Describe your fears about gaining weight, but remember, the average patient gains only a couple of pounds as a result of this treatment.

The Overweight Patient

If you are overweight and have bulimia nervosa, you may not feel anxious about small weight gains, but you may have unrealistic notions regarding weight loss. It is important that you not start restricting your diet again if you gain some weight during treatment. Doing so can lead to a relapse in binge eating and purging. If you are overweight and hoping to lose weight during treatment, just remember that the cycle of dieting, binge eating, and purging has not worked to maintain your weight and has been accompanied by much misery in terms of your preoccupation with food, anxiety, and guilt. The sensible alternative is to eat regularly, not to diet, and to adhere to a sensible exercise program. It has been our clinical experience that if you are overweight, you may exhibit a tendency to lose some weight if you adhere to the recommendations of this program, including establishing a regular pattern of eating moderately portioned meals and snacks at regular intervals throughout the day. Cognitive restructuring is another component of the program and can help you more easily accept your body weight and shape.

For the Binge-Eating Patient

Evidence suggests that you must resolve your binge eating before you have a chance to maintain your weight losses. If you are an overweight binge eater, you have a greater tendency to gain weight during cognitive-behavioral treatment. To prevent this, we suggest that some elements of a weight-control program be added to the first phase of the cognitive-behavioral therapy program. These include weekly weighing (as for patients with bulimia nervosa) to track any weight gains, a mild exercise program, and gradual dietary-fat reduction, consistent with American Heart Association guidelines that suggest only 30% of total calories come from fat. These elements appear to stop substantial weight gain during the course of cognitive-behavioral therapy.

Once you complete cognitive-behavioral therapy and stop binge eating, you should then move on to a behavioral weight-loss program while continuing the elements of cognitive-behavioral therapy. The aim here is to achieve a sensible lifestyle without dietary restriction. This program may lead to average weight losses of 13–15 lbs. Unlike weight lost through extreme diets or purging behaviors, these weight losses can be maintained as long as you abstain from binge eating. Returning to binge eating will cause weight gain. Research has shown that non-bingers have lost an average of 30 lbs more than bingers after one year. If you are unable to stop binge eating, alternative approaches to help you will be discussed in Chapter 6.

Summary

This chapter presented information about the medical complications of bulimia nervosa and binge-eating disorder, specifically the effects of purging, consuming large amounts of food at once, and maintaining a weight that is either higher or lower than the recommended range.

Homework

✎ Remember to complete your Daily Food Records.

✎ Continue to weigh yourself once a week and record your weight in the comments column of your Daily Food Record.

✎ Review chapters or sections of chapters as recommended by your therapist.

Self-Assessment

Take some time to review the contents of this chapter and complete the following self-assessment. Answer by filling in the correct words or phrases. Answers can be found in the Appendix.

1. Name some of the medical complications that can result from bulimia nervosa.

    _____

    _____

    _____

    _____

2. Name some of the medical complications of binge-eating disorder.

    _____

    _____

    _____

    _____

3. Describe the best strategy of withdrawal from laxatives.

    _____

    _____

    _____

    _____

Chapter 6

Measuring Your Progress: Refining or Revising Your Strategy

Goals

- To assess your progress in treatment and to consider the next steps in your recovery

Review of Previous Chapter

The information presented in Chapters 1–5 provided you with the basic elements of cognitive-behavioral therapy for bulimia and binge-eating disorder. You will recall that the primary interventions include regularly monitoring food intake and situational factors related to eating in detail, working toward a regular pattern of eating (having three meals and two snacks at specific times), weighing yourself weekly, and participating in pleasurable alternative activities. For binge-eating patients, interventions also include reducing fat intake and increasing exercise. By this point, you should be using these strategies regularly. If you are finding it difficult to follow through with these recommendations, you should discuss this with your therapist. Remember to continue using your Daily Food Records to record your eating. You should also weigh yourself weekly and record your weight in the comments column of the Daily Food Record.

Overview

Now that you are approximately one third of the way through the program, you may want to take some time to reflect upon the changes you have made in treatment. Have the interventions been helpful to you? If so, to what extent have they helped you? If not, why not, and what additional steps are needed? This chapter will help you assess your progress thus far and consider the next steps in your recovery.

How do you know if you're making progress in treatment? Which signs of improvement are the most important? One of the most important things for you to do in the first phase of therapy is to accept the cognitive-behavioral model of binge eating as a plausible explanation for your eating problems. The model draws a link between dietary restriction, negative moods, overemphasis on weight and shape, and binge eating. Interventions based on the model are designed to decrease tendencies to diet or restrict food intake in any way and reduce the influence of negative mood states and shape and weight concerns on eating behavior. Your openness to accepting some version of the model as an explanation for your eating problems implies a willingness to "risk" making the necessary behavioral improvements to your eating behavior. Alternatively, if you have misgivings about the model, this may suggest that you are still a little resistant to making the recommended changes in your eating pattern. You may also be unwilling to deal with the possible "negative consequences" of regular eating. In terms of assessing your progress, consider the extent to which the model illustrates aspects of your struggle with an eating disorder and associated problems. Along with "accepting" the model, you should agree to continue recording your food intake to gather as much data about your eating patterns as possible.

You should also look for significant changes in the central components of your eating disorder, such as a reduction in the number of your binge-and-purge episodes per week. In thinking about your strategies for decreasing these episodes, consider the extent to which you have reorganized your meal pattern so that you are eating three meals and two snacks per day at regular intervals. Adhering to a regular eating pattern has been shown to correspond with an improvement in binge eating. Regularizing your eating should be one of your primary tools for change. Your improved eating behaviors should also reflect the development of a more realistic and accepting relationship with your weight, particularly as represented by the numbers on the scale. A change of this nature may be evidenced by your capacity to tolerate a regimen of weekly weighing and to accept minor weight fluctuations as normal, without exaggerating the meaning of the numbers on the scale or using them to rationalize a return to dieting. If you are overweight or binge eating without purging, your program includes increased exercise and a reduction in dietary fat intake. These behaviors should also be rated when assessing your progress. More generally, it is important to ask yourself about the extent to which your sense of mastery and control over your eating behavior has increased during the treatment. Later in this chapter you will use progress-summary worksheets to help you quantify and document some of these changes. We also discuss alternative options you may want to try if you and your therapist feel that the first phase of therapy has not been as helpful as expected.

As you begin to consider the various areas of change and measure your response to treatment, you may be asking yourself if your rate of progress has been satisfactory. This chapter will provide you with some information to help you realistically view your progress. At the same time, keep in mind that whatever the "results" of your assessment, the very *process* of reviewing your progress is an extremely valuable learning experience for many reasons. Your interest in measuring your response to treatment reflects a continuation of the "scientific" approach toward your recovery that you've taken since beginning treatment. What this means is that you have become a thorough observer of yourself and the environmental factors that contribute to your overeating episodes and have started to experiment with the strategies recommended. You can use this chapter as an opportunity to summarize your progress and make thoughtful decisions about which direction to take in treatment. Based on the information collected in your summary and through discussion with your therapist, you will be able to determine the extent to which various strategies have been helpful, the degree to which the remaining problem areas warrant attention, and more broadly, the next steps to be taken in treatment. Your therapist will be especially helpful in considering the usefulness of reviewing or repeating Phase 1 of treatment, moving ahead to Phase 2, or shifting gears altogether.

Returning to the mechanics of measuring progress and change, it is important that you keep the "experimental" frame of reference in mind throughout your evaluation. This means being very specific in the way you think about your progress and taking care to accurately measure change in the *appropriate areas*. Given the tendency of individuals with eating disorders to exhibit certain thinking patterns (which will be addressed in Chapter 11) that prevent accurate appraisal of many situations, including their progress in treatment, it is particularly important for you to be as objective, specific, and accurate as possible. This includes very thoughtfully deciding which "outcome measures" are the best or most relevant to use in your progress evaluation.

Some of the thinking errors that may affect your appraisal of your progress can include the following:

Perfectionism. Judging yourself harshly and with much self-criticism if you fall short of some self-generated, ideal standard. For example, expecting yourself to eat by the prescribed pattern *every single day without fail,* and feeling like a failure if you don't.

Magnifying Negatives, Minimizing Positives. Focusing more on your personal shortcomings than on your strengths. For example, paying a lot more attention to the fact that you are still binge eating twice weekly rather than the fact that the frequency of your binges per week has decreased by 80%, or focusing on the discomfort you still experience when "feeling full" rather than the fact that in many instances you are finding it easy to tolerate the kind of normal fullness that comes from a pattern of regular meals and snacks.

Underestimating External Difficulties and Amplifying the Internal Deficiencies. That is, failing to consider how difficult it is to overcome an eating disorder and instead focusing on your "lack of willpower" to explain difficulties you've encountered during treatment.

Interpreting Events in All-or-Nothing Terms. That is, assuming that having some difficulty normalizing your meal pattern on some occasions means you are a "treatment failure" or that you will *never* be able to eat this way on a regular basis. Individuals with eating disorders expect very much from themselves, very quickly. You are probably similar in not cutting yourself much slack and not demonstrating a lot of patience, particularly with yourself. Likely, these attitudes extend to your views of your own therapy, especially how well you are doing in it and how quickly you are improving. Again, your therapist can be extremely helpful in correcting any biased impressions you might have of yourself and providing a more objective and realistic view of your progress.

Let's revisit the key areas of change you will use to estimate the effectiveness of your treatment to date.

Areas of Change in Therapy

- Establishing a regular eating pattern of three meals and two snacks a day

- Maintaining a pattern of once-weekly weighing

- Frequently engaging in pleasurable alternative activities instead of binge eating

- Experiencing a general sense of increased mastery and control over eating

- If overweight, establishing a regular exercise regimen

- If overweight, decreasing fat intake

Maintaining a Regular Eating Pattern

To determine how successful you have been in establishing a regular eating pattern, compare your current Daily Food Records to those from the beginning of treatment. The original records represent your baseline. First, compare the number of meals and snacks eaten per week. (It should be easy to identify your meals because you enclosed them in parentheses.) Then, compare the two sets of records for the number of days during which you've eaten *at least* three meals and two snacks. (Note: Some individuals may have been instructed by their therapist to make certain adaptations to the recommended pattern, such as including an additional snack or possibly eating fewer times a day.) In summarizing your progress, refer to the areas of change that have been most relevant to your therapy. Your therapist can help you tailor the indices of change if needed. For example, if you have been working to counteract a pattern of "grazing," you might want to include an assessment of the number of days on which you limited yourself to exactly three meals and two snacks, or had no more than six eating episodes, and so on.

Current number of meals per week		_____
minus	−	
Number of meals per week in first week		_____
equals	=	
Increase in number of meals per week		[ ]
Current number snacks per week		_____
minus	−	
Number of snacks per week in first week		_____
equals	=	
Increase in number of snacks per week		[ ]
Number of days eating at least 3 meals and 2 snacks in current week		_____
minus	−	
Number of days eating at least 3 meals and 2 snacks in first week		_____
equals	=	
Increase in number of days per week eating 3 meals and 2 snacks		[ ]

Weighing Yourself Weekly

To measure your response to the recommendation of once-weekly weighing, note the number of weeks since beginning treatment that you have weighed yourself weekly:

Number of weeks weighed one time: _____

Engaging in Pleasant, Alternative Activities

Think about when and how you have used alternative activities instead of binge eating. Estimate the number of times per week you are engaging in pleasurable alternative activities as an attempt to delay or prevent an overeating episode.

Current number of pleasurable
activities per week _____

minus —

Number of pleasurable activities
per week in first week _____

equals =

Increase in number of pleasurable
activities per week [   ]

Exercising and Reducing Fat Intake

If you are overweight, compare the number of days per week you are currently exercising with the number of days you exercised per week at the start of treatment. Also, rate the degree to which you have reduced your fat intake, using a 1–5 scale, where 1 represents much worsening, 2 represents some worsening, 3 represents no change, 4 represents some improvement, and 5 represents much improvement.

Current number of days
per week exercised _____

minus —

Number of days exercised
in first week _____

equals =

Increase in number of days
per week exercised [   ]

```
I————2————3————4————5
much worse      no change      much better
```

Rating for estimated reduction in fat intake [   ]

Mastering Eating

Finally, a more subjective assessment considers your sense of mastery and control over your eating. Spend some time thinking about your recent experience of eating and how it may contrast with the way you felt about eating before beginning treatment. Consider rating the degree of change on a 1–5 scale. You might also want to write a paragraph about how your experience of eating has changed. Again, discuss your thoughts with your therapist.

```
I————2————3————4————5
much worse      no change      much better
```

Overall sense of mastery in managing eating situations: _____

General thoughts about changes in the way you experience eating:

_____

_____

_____

_____

_____

_____

Summarize your progress data using the worksheet provided.

Number of meals per week in first week [   ]

Current number of meals per week [   ]

Number of snacks per week in first week [   ]

Current number of snacks per week [   ]

Number of days eating at least 3 meals
and 2 snacks in first week [   ]

Number of days eating at least 3 meals and 2 snacks in current week	
Increase in number of days per week eating 3 meals and 2 snacks	
Number of weeks weighed one time	
Number of pleasurable activities per week in first week	
Current number of pleasurable activities per week	
Overall rating of mastery in managing eating situations	

If You Exercise Too Much

Number of days per week exercised in first week	
Current number of days per week exercised	

A Note About Weight

You may have noticed that weight or weight changes are not a formal aspect of the progress evaluation, even for the overweight or binge-eating patient. Again, weight loss (or gain) is not an objective of this treatment program. In fact, in relation to the goal of weight loss, particularly for binge-eating patients, when this is appropriate, research studies suggest that a program targeting binge eating and paying some attention to fat content, portion control, and exercise will naturally lead to weight loss, if loss is desirable.

Now that you've completed an assessment of your progress during Phase 1 of treatment, you probably want to know what the assessment means and how your rate of progress compares to that of others. There is no specific expectation about the degree of change that you should have experienced by this point. Also, there is no way to compare yourself meaningfully to others undergoing the same treatment because every individual is unique. Each person undergoing treatment for an eating disorder presents with slightly different problems that respond differently to the treatment. However, we can say that individuals who are going to benefit from this program usually begin to respond successfully to Phase 1 at some point before or around Session 10. To determine how effective your treatment has been and will continue to be, you should discuss your progress summary with your therapist.

What are the signs that the treatment is not working? The first is that your progress worksheets show little or no improvement. Your lack of response may suggest that the cognitive-behavioral model does not apply to your eating problem and that this treatment approach has not helped you interrupt the cycle of binge eating and purging. Alternatively, you may have been too afraid about the consequences of regular eating, including the potential for weight gain, to really test the model and follow through with the recommendations to eat more regularly. You may feel that there are still too many benefits associated with binge eating and purging. Perhaps other pressing issues have interfered with your ability to focus on this treatment. You may also have realized that you are not ready or motivated at this time to make the kinds of behavior changes required.

Some additional factors are worth considering in attempting to understand the reasons that treatment is not working. Bulimic or binge-eating individuals who share certain of the following characteristics may have more difficulty in treatment compared to those who present with fewer complications. The list of such characteristics includes but is not limited to severe depression, active and excessive use of alcohol or other substances, sensitivity to perceived "authority" figures (even well-intentioned therapists), and/or other complicated personality variables.

After reviewing the summary of your progress, discuss with your therapist your feelings and perceptions about the therapy and how it's been going. Together you will decide whether or not there is a need to review or repeat the treatment methods presented so far, add additional methods, or switch to an entirely new approach. If you decide to switch gears, be reassured that there are other treatment approaches that are known to be effective in treating bulimia nervosa and binge-eating disorder. These include adding a medication (e.g., an antidepressant like Prozac) or considering an alternative form of therapy such as interpersonal psychotherapy (IPT) or emotion-regulation therapy (dialectical behavior therapy [DBT]), with or without medication. Your therapist will be familiar with these options and he or she will also be able to provide advice and encouragement about the usefulness of staying with this program, adding medication, or making the switch to another treatment approach.

Summary

This chapter provided information about a mid-treatment assessment of your progress. We encouraged you to take the time to review your response to treatment upon completing the first phase of the program, which focuses on behavior change, given our observation that significant improvements are typically evidenced by around Session 10. Several domains for assessing your progress were proposed, including maintaining a regular eating pattern, adhering to a regimen of once-weekly weighing, participating in pleasurable alternative activities, and enjoying a greater sense of mastery and control over eating. A general trend toward improvement in these domains and an overall feeling of having benefited from the program should guide your decisions about the next steps in your treatment. Keep in mind that a discussion with your therapist is essential to determine the nature of any refinements or revisions to your program. Review your progress again before going on to the next chapter.

Homework

✎ Complete the summary of progress worksheets included in this chapter.

✎ Discuss your progress and general experience in the program with your therapist. Based on this discussion, agree upon a plan of action as described in the chapter.

✎ Continue all aspects of the program (keeping Daily Food Records, working toward a regular eating pattern, and engaging in pleasurable alternative activities). Continue to weigh yourself once a week and record your weight in the comments column of your Daily Food Record.

Self-Assessment

Take some time to review the contents of this chapter and complete the following self-assessment. Answer by filling in the correct words or phrases, or by circling T (True) or F (False). Answers can be found in the Appendix.

1. Name some of the different outcomes that you should take into account in considering your response to treatment.

    _____

    _____

    _____

    _____

2. Individuals with eating disorders tend to be self-critical when thinking about their progress in treatment.   T   F

3. Name the types of interpretive errors that individuals with eating disorders tend to make in assessing their own performance (for example, when measuring their response to treatment).

_____

_____

_____

_____

4. What options do you have if you feel that the treatment is not working?

_____

_____

_____

_____

Chapter 7

Feared and Problem Foods

Goals

- To make a list of foods you fear and avoid

- To begin incorporating your least-feared foods into your daily eating routine

Review of Previous Chapter

You should be continuing with all aspects of the program. Remember to complete Daily Food Records and note all factors that contribute to any problematic eating episodes. Make an effort to eat more regularly and engage in pleasurable alternative activities to delay or prevent overeating episodes. You should also be weighing yourself weekly, noting your weight in the comments column of your Daily Food Record.

Overview

In this chapter you will be presented with a rationale for beginning to consume foods that you might avoid because you think these foods are "bad" or "off limits." We will discuss a method for identifying these kinds of foods and incorporating them into your meal plan.

What Is a Feared Food?

If you are like others with bulimia nervosa, it's likely that the number of foods you actually feel comfortable eating normally and keeping down (as opposed to bingeing and purging) is quite small. You might even be able to name in a matter of just a few minutes all the foods that you regularly eat. At the same time, you have probably developed a very long list of "bad" or "feared" foods that you attempt to avoid. You may regard these foods as being fattening or too caloric, or having too much fat. Likely, you try to follow very strict rules concerning your intake of such foods, perhaps believing that they should *never* be eaten or that they should be eaten only in very small amounts or only in special circumstances, such as at a particular time of day or a specific type of gathering. Ironically, these same foods may be the foods most likely to trigger or prolong a binge. Why is that so?

It is important to question yourself about your rationale for identifying certain foods as "bad" or "off limits" so that you can understand the origin, nature, and extent of your food avoidance. When you avoid or deprive yourself of foods you naturally like and crave, you are setting yourself up to overindulge on those foods later. Basically, these foods become more attractive and tempting the more you deny yourself access to them, thus resulting in a loss of control in the form of a binge. Similarly, when you find yourself in the midst of a bingeing episode, you may reach for these foods first. Also, keep in mind that avoiding anything feared will strengthen your fear. The longer you avoid feared foods, the more exaggerated your worries about them will become. Finally, remember that removing your feared foods from your diet is just another form of restriction, and any form of strict dieting increases your risk for binge eating.

The following brief interaction between Sue and her therapist illustrates the issues surrounding avoidance of feared foods.

S: Last week, we went to Max's again. The week before when we went there, I ordered what I really wanted. But last night I didn't order what I wanted.

T: What did you really want, and why didn't you order it?

S: I wanted the cheesy garlic bread; I was craving it again, but I still wouldn't let myself order it.

T: And you didn't order it because?

S: I gotta get into this tight little dress.

T: And cheesy garlic bread is fattening. What did you order instead?

S: A little bit of salad and a piece of bread with turkey. A low-calorie meal. And I was hungry and doggone it if I didn't have two cookies and candy bars later.

T: And threw up?

S: Yup. It was a good experiment to do this. Compared to the week before, I had my cheesy garlic bread and salad. I was happy. No problem afterward.

T: What did you learn?

S: In addition to cutting back physically, I was cutting back emotionally, psychologically wanting to eat.

T: Yes. I guess what I'm hearing is that when you deprive yourself you end up paying later. You wanted the garlic bread, not to put words in your mouth, but perhaps there were some of those fears around food contents. If I eat a food like this, I will gain weight, and I won't fit in that dress. Therefore, I have to restrict myself.

S: That's exactly what I was thinking because I tried on the dress the night before.

Considering the issues raised in this example, the solution becomes fairly obvious. The best way to stop tempting yourself to overindulge on feared foods is to begin to eat them occasionally and in moderation. Doing this will help you learn to trust yourself and your body to regulate your food intake.

Identifying Feared Foods

Ideally, you should complete this exercise at a grocery store, where you can easily be reminded of the many types of foods you automatically label as bad or off limits. The initial objective is to heighten your awareness of the extent of your food avoidance. First, take a pad of paper and a pen to the store and note all the "feared" or "off-limits" foods you notice. At home, use the Feared and Problem Foods List provided to group the foods into four categories. Category 1 represents foods that you fear the least, and Category 4 represents foods you fear the most.

Introducing Feared Foods into Your Diet

The second aim of the exercise is to introduce small quantities of feared foods into your meal plan. We recommend you approach this task using the same small-steps method you have used throughout this program. The first foods you introduce should come from the least-feared category (Category 1). Attempt to include one or two of these foods in your diet each week. It is best to plan to experiment with eating these foods in a controlled, non-stressful environment in which portion sizes can be easily managed using external constraints of one type or another (e.g., the amount is limited, or people are around), and from which there is little opportunity to escape for a purge. Give yourself some extra credit for trying these feared foods by identifying them with an asterisk (*) in your food records. Also, take note of any thoughts or feelings you become aware of before or after you eat any of these feared foods. As you become more comfortable with a food, remember to cross it off your list! Most likely, you will progress through the categories, from least to most difficult, slowly over time, although some individuals are so quickly able to comprehend the "safety" of these formerly feared foods that they might start skipping ahead and quickly mastering many more foods than they ever expected. Many report the experience of "rediscovering" their relationship with foods they previously enjoyed and felt "safe" with before their eating disorder developed—an experience that is very exciting to be part of!

It is not uncommon to initially experience distinct or persistent problem thoughts related to these feared foods. For example, you might start to think about the effects of these foods on your weight and shape in a catastrophic way. You may also think that you will need to purge after eating feared foods. Remind yourself that you are viewing these foods through the lens of your eating disorder. It is likely that your thoughts regarding these foods are exaggerated and

Feared and Problem Foods List

Category 1 (least feared)	Category 2	Category 3	Category 4 (most feared)

distorted. In Chapter 11, you will learn a method to track and challenge troubling thoughts of this nature. In the meantime, it is important for you to find a way to reassure yourself during this process of experimentation. The following information might be helpful. Keep in mind that eating small or moderate amounts of a particular food will not have a drastic effect on your weight or shape. Furthermore, interrupting a pattern of strict dieting by eating a wider variety of foods (and maintaining a regular pattern of eating, as already discussed) is the surest way to prevent or decrease the frequency and size of your binge-eating episodes. Remember, binge eating will always contribute excess calories to your diet. As discussed in Chapter 4, purging is not an effective way of getting rid of the excess calories consumed in a binge. Finally, rest assured! We are not necessarily encouraging you to eat all your feared foods regularly, but rather to develop a sense of flexibility, mastery, and control over all foods and food groups so that you can eat any food in normal quantities without experiencing undue anxiety or distress. Again, the rationale for incorporating these feared foods into your meal plan stems from the cognitive-behavioral model of eating disorders. Eliminating specific foods and food groups from your diet represents a form of dieting and, as you know by now, all forms of dieting can lead to binge eating. Thus, by adding feared foods to your meal plan, you are taking another step that combats the vicious cycle of dieting, binge eating, and purging.

For the Binge-Eating Patient

As a binge eater, you are less likely than a bulimic to engage in dietary restriction and more likely to eat frequently and to consume a wider variety of foods. You probably don't identify as many foods as bad or off limits as a bulimic does, but you may be equally likely to identify "problematic" or trigger foods that lead to binges or are included in your overeating or binge episodes. Incorporating these problematic foods into your diet is as important for you as it is for the bulimic, but portion control and some element of "restriction" should be emphasized. You can accomplish these goals by better regulating the frequency and timing of your eating episodes. An example that illustrates good eating control would be to resist eating a few slices of chocolate cake at breakfast but allowing yourself to have a small piece of cake in a much more appropriate situation, such as for dessert after lunch or dinner. Also, in order to balance the inclusion of problematic foods into your meal plan with your other dietary goals such as the reduction of fat intake, you may want to limit consumption of these feared foods, especially when they are "indulgence"-type foods that are high in calories and fat. For example, you may want to limit yourself to eating this type of food once a week. In general, apply the overriding principles of moderation and flexibility when considering strategies for including feared foods in your diet.

Summary

The problem of off-limits foods was discussed with the assumption that you may avoid a number of "bad," but inherently enjoyable, foods that you probably like and crave. The issues of binge eaters and trigger foods were discussed from a slightly different angle. We presented a rationale and method for incorporating feared foods into your diet and made suggestions for heightening your awareness of the problem thoughts and feelings that may arise as you begin to experiment with feared foods. Binge eaters were encouraged to more strategically plan their consumption of these foods.

Homework

✎ Create your list of feared foods, grouping the foods into four categories, ranging from the least feared to the most feared.

✎ Include one or two of the least-feared foods in your diet this week.

✎ Continue all aspects of the program (keeping Daily Food Records, working toward a regular pattern of eating, and engaging in pleasurable alternative activities). Continue to weigh yourself once a week and record your weight in the comments column of your Daily Food Record.

Take some time to review the contents of this chapter and complete the following self-assessment. Answer by filling in the correct words or phrases, or by circling T (True) or F (False). Answers can be found in the Appendix.

1. Individuals with some eating disorders attempt to regularly deny themselves foods they like but then end up bingeing on these same foods.   T   F

2. What is the rationale for reintroducing feared or avoided foods into your diet?

    _____

    _____

    _____

    _____

3. What are the conditions that lead to the most success when consuming feared or trigger foods?

    _____

    _____

    _____

    _____

4. It is a good idea to avoid eating "problem foods" like sugar, chocolate, or pizza altogether.   T   F

Chapter 8   *Understanding Binge Triggers*

Goals

- ◼ To identify various types of binge triggers
- ◼ To learn strategies for monitoring and managing your triggers

Review of Previous Chapter

You should be continuing with all aspects of the program, including introducing feared or avoided foods into your meal plan. Remember to complete Daily Food Records and to note all factors that contribute to any problematic eating episodes. Make an effort to eat more regularly and use pleasant alternative activities to delay or prevent overeating episodes. You should also be weighing yourself weekly, noting your weight in the comments column of your Daily Food Record.

Be sure to review prior chapters to make certain that you understand and have basically mastered the material and suggested strategies before continuing.

Overview

We hope you have experienced some relief from binge eating in response to the behavior-change strategies introduced in the first phase of treatment. Whereas the first phase focused on eliminating dieting and hunger as a primary binge trigger, Phase 2 will help you become more aware of the remaining precipitants to your binge episodes, which may be mediated by your thoughts and emotions. This chapter will identify different types of binge triggers and introduce methods for monitoring and managing them.

By now, you have probably spent some time trying to figure out why you binge and purge. You should be using the comments column of your Daily Food Record regularly to record the factors that seem to be related to your binge-eating episodes, whether they are feelings, thoughts, or sensations of hunger. However, you may have noticed that in spite of your efforts to understand why you binge, it is often quite difficult to come up with an answer. This suggests that some of your binges occur for reasons that are as yet unclear. And that may be a problem if, like other individuals with eating disorders, you blame yourself for "being weak" or succumbing to a "lack of willpower" instead of recognizing that you have not collected enough data about binge triggers. It is important for you to recognize that typically *there are concrete factors unrelated to personal strength or willpower* that explain the occurrence of a binge-and-purge episode. This mind-set should help motivate you to search for and desire to change the actual triggering factors.

Think of a binge episode as occurring in a given situation or context. The context refers to any event—broadly defined—that has occurred in the minutes, hours, or in some cases even days, before or during a binge episode and that has had, or continues to have, an effect on you. When considering the context of any given binge or overeating episode, it is helpful to take into account the following three clusters of factors:

- *External factors*, including the place, time, and "atmosphere" of the eating episode, and the types and quantities of food available;

- *Social factors*, including the presence *or* absence of others, and the nature of interpersonal interactions with those who are present; and

- *Internal factors*, including your thoughts, feelings (and general level of "arousal"), and state of hunger or satiety.

Once you understand these factors, you will be better able to figure out why you binged and will be able to anticipate and plan better strategies for preventing binges when these factors are present.

To heighten your awareness of your own primary binge triggers, think about your most recent bingeing episodes. You may want to refer to past Daily Food Records to jog your memory. Use the space provided to list the factors that seem to have been most prominent in increasing your risk for bingeing.

Identifying Binge Triggers

Let's start with the external factors. Ask yourself the following questions. Where were you when you binged? What time of day or night was it? Which foods were available and in what quantities? Jot down some ideas about the external factors that seem to be linked to your binge episodes.

Triggers from the External Environment

1. _____

2. _____

3. _____

4. _____

5. _____

Next, examine the social factors. Consider the following: Were you alone or with others? Who was present, and how would you characterize your general relationship with this person and the nature of the interaction around the time of your binge? Was there any type of interpersonal conflict that might have affected you? Record your impressions of the significant social triggers.

Triggers from the Social Environment

1. _____

2. _____

3. _____

4. _____

5. _____

Finally, consider the internal factors. First, put these into three separate groups: thoughts, feelings (including your general level of "arousal"), and your state of hunger or satiety.

Let's take hunger and satiety first. How hungry were you at or around the time that you binged? If you were not aware of feeling hungry, had there been a pattern of dietary restriction in the hours or days before your binge that might have contributed in some way? Had you recently overeaten then *intended* to restrict your eating but violated your rules about what you should or shouldn't eat, leading you to binge? Record the aspects of your experience of hunger that seem to be related to your binges.

Triggers from the Internal Environment (Hunger)

1. _____

2. _____

3. _____

4. _____

5. _____

Next, let's look at strong feeling states, both positive and negative, and general level of arousal. Consider the following: How were you feeling and what was your general mood before (during, and after) your binge? Did you eat in an attempt to tone down or distract yourself from feelings (either positive or negative) that were too strong? Was eating an attempt to experience pleasure or enjoyment? Or, knowing that you'd feel worse after eating, was it a form of self-punishment? Jot down some notes regarding the connection between your feelings and your binges.

Triggers from the Internal Environment (Feelings)

1. _____

2. _____

3. _____

4. _____

5. _____

The third aspect of internal factors pertains to your thoughts. In identifying the thoughts that may play a role in your binge episodes, consider the following: What were you thinking about before, during, or after your binge? Were the thoughts positive or negative? Did the nature of your thoughts change as a result of the binge; for example, did you binge to shift your focus from negative thoughts to thoughts about eating? Were you thinking critically about food, eating, or your body, for example, exaggerating the amounts you had consumed or the possibility that you might gain weight based on what you had consumed? Were you dwelling on a specific, recurrent troubling thought, such as a preoccupation or over-concern with some aspect of your body shape or physical appearance or confusion about how to resolve a problem in your life? List the ways in which your thoughts have been related to your binge-eating episodes.

Triggers from the Internal Environment (Thoughts)

1. _____

2. _____

3. _____

4. _____

5. _____

The following chart was designed to help you summarize the information you've obtained regarding your most prominent binge triggers. List the primary binge triggers you identified above in the appropriate categories.

We hope this exercise has helped you identify the primary external, social, and internal factors associated with your tendency to binge. The next step is to develop a set of interventions to help you control the influence of these factors on your eating. The next few chapters will introduce methods to solve problem situations and challenge troubling thoughts, specifically concerns about body shape and weight. Remember, you've already learned the most helpful intervention—eliminating dieting by eating regularly and incorporating a wide range of foods into your diet. Also, you have already learned the advantages of referring to a list of pleasurable alternative

Summary of Factors that Contribute to Binges

External Factors	Social Factors	Internal Factors		
		Hunger	Feelings	Thoughts

activities as a method for delaying or preventing binges. Engaging in a pleasurable alternative activity can be particularly helpful when binges are triggered by negative moods and boredom. Take some time to review and expand your list of pleasurable alternative activities, keeping in mind that these activities can help you offset the effects of a negative mood. The role of negative moods and interpersonal interactions in precipitating binge episodes will be revisited in Chapter 12.

Summary

This chapter discussed three general types of triggering factors that may increase your risk for binge eating. Three categories were described: external factors, social factors, and internal factors, including hunger, thoughts, and feelings. You were given an opportunity, through a review of your most recent food records, to identify the factors that seem to be the most salient binge triggers for you. This chapter included a brief review of the methods for coping with these triggers that were introduced earlier in the program, namely, eating regularly to avoid extreme hunger, and engaging in pleasurable alternative activities to offset the influence of a negative mood. Additional methods for challenging problem thoughts and resolving problem situations will be introduced in the next few chapters.

Homework

✎ Complete all the exercises in this chapter.

✎ If you have not been doing this so far, use the comments column of your Daily Food Record to take note of the factors triggering your binge episodes.

✎ Review and expand your list of pleasurable alternative activities to specifically address high-risk situations that trigger negative moods and boredom.

✎ Continue all aspects of the program (keeping Daily Food Records, working toward a regular pattern of eating, and engaging in pleasurable alternative activities). Continue to weigh yourself once a week and record your weight in the comments column of your Daily Food Record.

Self-Assessment

Take some time to review the contents of this chapter and complete the following self-assessment. Answer by filling in the correct words or phrases. Answers can be found in the Appendix.

1. Name three different types of "internal factors" that might trigger your binges.

    _____

    _____

    _____

    _____

2. What can you do to minimize the effects of factors that increase your risk for bingeing?

    _____

    _____

    _____

    _____

3. Many individuals with eating disorders err on the side of attributing their binges to (external or internal) _____ factors.

4. Eating regularly minimizes the effects of which type of triggering factor?

    _____

    _____

    _____

    _____

Chapter 9   *Weight and Shape Concerns*

Goals

- To discuss your concerns about weight and shape and the role they play in your eating disorder

- To learn methods for identifying, monitoring, and reducing the types of body-checking behaviors you perform each day

Review of Previous Chapter

You should be continuing with all aspects of the program. Remember to complete the Daily Food Records and note all factors that contribute to any problematic eating episodes. Make an effort to eat more regularly and use pleasurable alternative activities to delay or prevent overeating episodes. You should also be weighing yourself weekly, noting your weight in the comments column of your Daily Food Record.

Periodically review the earlier chapters to ensure that you understand each topic and are able to correctly use the recommended procedures.

Overview

This chapter will discuss your concerns about weight and shape and their role in the development and maintenance of your eating disorder. Body-image concerns are characteristic of individuals with eating disorders and often continue long after resolution of the disordered eating behaviors. Since specific worries about weight and shape or a general preoccupation with the body can precipitate binge-eating episodes, a method for challenging these concerns should be a part of your binge-prevention strategy. Several issues related to body image will be addressed in this chapter, including (a) overvalued ideas regarding the importance of weight and shape; (b) negative beliefs about your body stemming from critical comments from others and teasing about weight or physical appearance; (c) preoccupation with the body as a form of distraction from other important issues; (d) exaggerated fears of weight gain following implementation of a normal pattern of eating; and (e) avoidance of certain pleasurable activities because of weight and shape concerns. Finally, strategies to interrupt and challenge negative body-image attitudes and behaviors will be presented. These will include six methods for identifying, monitoring, and reducing the types of body-checking behaviors you perform each day as a result of your body-image concerns.

The Role of Body-Image Concerns in the Development of an Eating Disorder

One of the factors individuals with eating disorders most often mention when asked why they diet or restrict their food intake is that they are worried about their shape and weight. If this sounds like you, you may fear that eating normally will lead inevitably to excessive weight gain. Although you may accept your worries as normal reactions to *real* physical changes, we know that body-image concerns are usually based on distorted perceptions driven to some extent by low self-esteem. You may have started feeling bad about yourself because of problems encountered during development. Many bulimics report that they were teased about fatness, regarded as overweight by their families and peers, given confusing messages that equated eating with overindulgence, and so on. Moreover, in the Western world today, the social pressure to achieve a thin and firm body shape of certain, culturally sanctioned proportions—quite impossible for most women—gives rise to body dissatisfaction even in many women who do not have eating disorders. What this means is that most women in our culture have some concerns about their body shape and weight. In addition, even individuals who have recovered from the behavioral aspects of an eating disorder and who have learned to challenge and question prescriptions for how they should look may find that their body-image concerns, although diminished in intensity, persist to some degree after they successfully complete therapy. Hence, it is important for you to realize that it will not be possible to totally eliminate your concerns about weight and shape. Rather, a heightened awareness and consistent use of the strategies presented in this chapter should help allay your concerns significantly.

Body-Image Distortion

Individuals with eating disorders such as bulimia or binge-eating disorder perceive their bodies with a level of distortion that falls on a continuum from *somewhat* to *quite significantly* distorted. To what extent is your body image distorted? Do you exaggerate the meaning of small changes in your weight or aspects of your body shape that displease you? Are you convinced of the factual nature of your concerns, despite objective evidence to the contrary, such as maintaining an average weight, being able to fit into average-sized clothing, or receiving consistent, favorable feedback about your body from others? Do others comment on the high level of self-criticism with which you describe your body? To illustrate what it is like to live with an extremely negative body image, let's revisit the therapy of Sue, the patient described earlier in this workbook.

Sue had been overweight as a child and adolescent, and her eating was constantly controlled and monitored by her mother, who was also overweight. In fact, she and her mother dieted together and both used diet pills. Sue saw herself as overweight and unattractive, despite the fact that later in her life she was able to lose a significant amount of weight (and it was in that process that she developed a full-blown eating disorder). Her self-concept also included the idea that her eating habits and weight were, and always would be, "out of control." When Sue first entered treatment, it became clear that no matter the level of improvement in her eating-disordered behaviors, the negative feelings and beliefs about her body persisted. Specifically, despite the fact that her weight was in the "low–normal" range for her height, she remained convinced that she had a "thick middle." She also sustained a level of dissatisfaction with her breasts that had worsened since divorcing and subsequently reentering the dating world. The fact that she was constantly fatigued and, as a result, unable to exercise much or to otherwise enjoy the physical activities she had enjoyed in the past (e.g., dancing) to stay in shape did not help her with respect to her body image. Nonetheless, her boyfriend often told her how physically attractive she was. In addition, her physician constantly reminded her that her weight was, if anything, a bit too low.

Like Sue, you may struggle with concerns about your body shape and weight that fall somewhere on the continuum between some level of dissatisfaction and total unacceptability. This chapter will present information and recommendations that should help you re-align your body image to be more consistent with reality. This chapter will also help you move beyond a place where you are overvaluing physical appearance to the extent that you have been. You will be given an opportunity to think about the types of situations that foster your weight and shape concerns, learn more about the reasons you may become preoccupied with your body in certain situations, and figure out strategies for working through the body-image concerns that persist. As you read and work on the exercises in this chapter, keep in mind a few points. First, as previously stated, it is important to remember that although you can expect your weight and shape concerns to diminish somewhat after working on the issues in therapy, it is reasonable to anticipate that, as a woman in our culture, your concerns about your body will persist to some degree. Ultimately, you may have to develop a strategy to coexist with them, rather than obliterate them entirely. Second, you must also accept that as someone who has had an eating disorder, you are unable to accurately judge your body. Rather, think of your skills as similar to those of a color-blind person attempting to distinguish between red and green. It can't be done. Therefore, it is important *just for now* to avoid drawing any definite conclusions about the weight and shape aspects of your physical appearance. Again, think of Sue, who was so convinced of her physical flaws that she would not even take seriously the perspectives of other people who loved her or the data provided by her physician, who was referring to commonly accepted weight charts. You will be doing yourself a favor to accept just for now that you don't have the capacity to see your body realistically. You need to withhold making judgments about your body until you possess the necessary skills.

Working on your body image requires you to become more aware of the specific thoughts and feelings involved and the situations that trigger them. Some of this information may have come to light earlier in therapy, when you examined the situations in which binge eating or other eating problems occurred. You may find that the situations that trigger negative body-image thoughts and feelings share themes related to some of the developmental issues mentioned earlier, such as having developed ideas that being thin is more important than it is or having been exposed at an early age to critical comments about your appearance or to confusing messages about what it means to satisfy your appetite; as a result, you may have come to equate eating with self-indulgence or selfishness. On the other hand, there may be current factors contributing to your negative body-image thoughts and feelings that seem relatively straightforward, for example, exposing your body when exercising, wearing a bathing suit at the beach, or being physically intimate with a romantic partner. Additional triggers may be subtler, such as focusing on your weight or body shape rather than facing more complicated emotions or interpersonal situations. You may feel that you can control your weight and shape through diet and exercise, whereas you may not be able to solve your personal problems. Finally, certain aspects of the treatment and recovery process itself, such as worrying about the "side effects" of consuming and keeping down regular meals and snacks (e.g., occasional bloating, fluid retention, and mild weight gain), can trigger worries about your body. Based on the specific issues you present in treatment, your therapist will help you develop as many strategies as possible to use to address your body-image concerns. By working hard in treatment to improve your body image, you are laying the foundation for your long-term recovery from bulimia.

In addition to heightening your awareness of the thoughts and feelings you have about your weight and shape, it is equally important to take note of the situations that contribute to your body-checking behaviors. These behaviors can lead to negative body perceptions as well. For example, many women with eating disorders report that check themselves each and every time they pass a window or mirror.

Other women use "pinching"-type behaviors to determine the amount of flesh or "fat" on various parts of their bodies, such as their upper arms, thighs, or stomach. They may unconsciously find themselves pinching or encircling these parts of their body in an attempt to measure or compare these parts from one occasion to the next, up to several times per day. The first step toward changing these behaviors is to record how frequently you do them before you make any attempt to change them. In fact, many individuals with eating disorders report feeling free and validated once they recognize that their seemingly involuntary and automatic body-checking behaviors have been part of their eating disorder all along. People often report some relief from the body-image distress soon after they begin working to decrease the frequency of their body-checking behaviors. You can use the form provided to identify the types of body-checking behaviors you engage in and the frequency of these behaviors.

Common Types of Body-Image Concerns and Suggested Interventions

Overvaluing a Slim Figure

Consider that cultural standards are arbitrary. When you think about the social and cultural pressures to be thin, consider that these standards are unpredictable and always changing. Focus on the fact that, over the years, different cultures have varied in what they have considered an attractive weight or shape. In many cultures, a rounded, softer, fuller body has been regarded as more feminine and attractive. Biologically, these standards are more realistic. Women need some body fat to retain good health and reproductive capabilities. Ask yourself to what extent you are willing to jeopardize your own health to live up to inappropriate cultural expectations about how you should look.

Identify and accentuate personal attributes unrelated to weight and shape. Begin to think more broadly about personal strengths that are unrelated to your weight and shape. These may include aspects of your character, your interests and activities, or your relationships. Also include valued aspects of your physical appearance that don't involve weight (e.g., hair, eyes, skin tone, hands, style of dress). Certainly, you

Body Checking Behaviors

Body Checking Behaviors

1. _____

2. _____

3. _____

4. _____

5. _____

6. _____

7. _____

8. _____

Frequency of Body Checking Behaviors

Behaviors	Mon	Tues	Wed	Thurs	Fri	Sat	Sun
1. _____							
2. _____							
3. _____							
4. _____							
5. _____							
6. _____							

notice far more than just weight and shape in evaluating the looks of another person; apply this same standard to yourself! Once you can identify personal attributes that you value, you can spend time further developing them instead of focusing on your weight and shape. Use the space provided to list your valued personal characteristics and physical attributes.

Valued Personal Characteristics (Unrelated to Physical Appearance, Weight, or Shape):

_____

_____

_____

_____

_____

Valued Physical Attributes (Unrelated to Weight or Shape):

_____

_____

_____

_____

_____

Make reasonable, desired changes in your appearance. If you are dissatisfied with your appearance in general, can you take some reasonable steps to improve it? For example, consider getting a new haircut, experimenting with makeup, or changing your style of dress. Doing this might improve the way you feel about your appearance. Go to a clothing store and ask a salesperson or close friend for advice in selecting styles in your size that are particularly flattering. Or, get a facial or makeover and ask for advice regarding your skin-care or cosmetics regimen.

Identify your physical assets by comparing yourself favorably to others. Collect some data about your physical-appearance concerns. You might discover that they are unfounded! Consider making use of opportunities to view your own figure in addition to the figures of other women, noting both assets and flaws, in a more realistic light, perhaps in a health club locker room. You will find that women come in various shapes and sizes, each with their inherent advantages and disadvantages. Comparing yourself to others might help you see that you have been exaggerating your perceived flaws and underestimating your assets.

Feeling "Fat," Based on Criticism or Other Concerns

Consider that feedback from the past is no longer relevant. As noted earlier in the chapter, many individuals with bulimia or binge-eating disorder have had a number of hurtful experiences concerning weight and shape over a long period, leading to a core belief that they are fat and unattractive in spite of objective evidence to the contrary. In some cases, their eating disorder might actually have begun in response to a critical comment about weight, such as overhearing a teasing remark in adolescence, or being called a name like "glutton" or "pig." Consider that these comments may have been untrue and unhelpful and are no longer applicable. Use your treatment experience as an opportunity to develop more-realistic and self-enhancing beliefs.

Separate weight concerns from other emotional or interpersonal problems. Beliefs about being fat or unshapely may become linked with general self-esteem concerns, interpersonal difficulties, and associated emotions (e.g., sadness, loneliness, guilt, anger), particularly if you are sensitive and prone to worrying about your self-worth and adequacy. Self-worth concerns then turn into worries about weight and shape, and dieting seems like a solution. This is how dieting and weight loss come to be viewed as a cure-all for your emotional upset. However, once you become aware of the association between heightened body-image concerns and other types of emotional or interpersonal issues, you can understand that if you are preoccupied with your body, *something else* may be wrong that warrants a solution other than dieting or weight loss.

To determine the root of the real problem, take note of specific situations in which you begin to dwell on your weight or shape concerns and record them in the log on page 129. Is it possible that your upset stems from a source other than your body? Question yourself in depth about what might *really* be going on. Are you experiencing a strained relationship with someone in your life? Is your mood generally low? Do you feel sad, lonely, or inadequate? Examine the costs and benefits of becoming preoccupied with your body. Will the worries about your body, or eVorts to diet, bring you closer to or take you farther from an actual solution to your problem? Keep in mind that "losing yourself" in critical observations about your body distracts you and allows you to escape from dealing with other stressors and "real-life" events, just the way binge eating and purging "numb" you to your feelings. Take a look at Sue's Weight and Shape Concerns Log shown in Figure 9.1 and use it as a model when filling out your own.

Triggering Situations and Events:	1. Boyfriend didn't call about plans for that night and feeling fat to begin with. 2. Too tired to get out that day and walk or exercise. 3. Low mood, feeling lonely.
Negative Thoughts and Beliefs:	1. I am fat and no one loves me. 2. My body is ugly. 3. Other than eating, there is nothing interesting to do because no one wants me around.
Consequences:	1. Sat at home and moped about how lonely and unattractive I am. 2. Was tempted to binge and purge. 3. Kept focusing on my body and my mood just got worse.
Methods of Coping:	Next time: 1. I would remind myself that my weight is in the normal range, no matter how I feel about it. The "data" places it in the range of normal. 2. I would realize that the real problem is not my weight or appearance but my mood and how I feel about myself and my loneliness. 3. I would try to come up with some more reasonable solutions, like thinking about some other people who might want to spend time with me or consider some interesting activities that I might want to try to do, even at home (e.g. reading magazines, doing a puzzle, giving myself a manicure, etc.). 4. No matter what, "getting out of my head" and getting off of the focus on body would have helped.

Figure 9.1 Sue's Weight and Shape Concerns Log

Weight and Shape Concerns Log

Examine a situation in which concerns about your weight and body shape may have been the catalyst for a binge episode. Write down your own trigger situation, negative thoughts, consequences, and alternative coping.

Triggering Situations and Events:	
Negative Thoughts and Beliefs:	
Consequences:	
Methods of Coping:	

Worrying About How Regular Eating Will Affect Your Weight and Shape

Remind yourself that regular eating is the best weight-management strategy. Many eating-disordered patients in recovery expect to gain weight when they stop their eating-disordered behaviors. You, too, may have worries or anxiety about the effects that normalizing your meal pattern will have on your weight and shape. Although there is the potential for minor weight gain during cognitive-behavioral therapy, for the most part, these worries represent perceptual distortions caused by your eating disorder. Experiment with different strategies to cope with these worries. You can learn to coexist with your worries by pushing them to the periphery of your awareness and acting "as if" you were satisfied with your body, by, for example, continuing to eat regular meals and snacks in spite of your fears of weight gain. You can also challenge these distorted beliefs by reviewing the model of binge eating presented in Chapter 4 and using the cognitive-restructuring methods presented in Chapter 11. The model shows that eating regular meals and snacks is an effective way to prevent binge episodes and maintain weight. This plan is supported by research results that show that binge eating leads to weight gain. Finally, keep in mind that purging is ineffective as a long-term weight-management tool. It leaves you feeling deprived, depleted, and at risk for additional binge eating.

Remember that your body will stabilize at a "natural weight" when you are treating it well by eating regularly. Your body will stabilize at a weight that can be maintained easily, without restricting or otherwise depriving yourself. If you have maintained your weight in this healthy range since beginning treatment, you should be reassured of this fact. If you have gained a few pounds since beginning treatment, consider the following. First, if you entered the program weighing less than you should, your weight gain may represent a "correction" to a weight that is more reasonable and healthier. Challenge any extreme thoughts or beliefs regarding your weight gain or your shape (e.g., "I'm going to continue to gain at least 5 lbs per month" or "Now I am as big as an elephant"), using the method presented in Chapter 11. Second, if you have gained more than the weight needed to put you in the healthy range, review the section about overvaluing being slim, question and challenge the significance of maintaining a slim shape, and work to accept the possibility that your weight might stabilize at a level that is higher than average. Remind yourself that your weight, no matter what range it falls within, is only one small part of you; there are undoubtedly other, more valuable, lovable, and significant parts. Examine the costs and benefits of gaining a few pounds as opposed to continuing to binge and purge. Is a slim physique really worth the physical and emotional costs associated with bulimia? Finally, if you are unhappy about your weight *and* you are maintaining a weight that is *substantially* higher than average, talk to your therapist. He or she will support your efforts to adopt an all-around healthy lifestyle plan that incorporates a moderate regimen of exercise and dietary interventions, such as portion control and reduction of fat intake, without dieting. A plan of this nature should help you improve your body image by enhancing your overall sense of well-being and control and by allowing for gradual weight loss to reach a healthy weight range.

Avoiding Activities in Which Your Body Will Be Exposed

Many individuals with eating disorders avoid potentially pleasurable activities because they are concerned about their shape or weight. Unfortunately, by avoiding these activities—like an evening date or a trip to the beach—which may be social or pleasurable, they are also forgoing opportunities to obtain potentially corrective feedback about their appearance, body shape, or weight. The time that could have been spent in an enjoyable activity may be spent alone, possibly worrying about or actually engaged in binge eating and purging.

Address the problem of activity avoidance as you have addressed the problem of feared foods. Just do it! The goal here is to help you regain your ability to enjoy a wide range of activities, regardless of your body size or shape. Participating in these potentially uncomfortable activities and situations will help you work through your fears and give you an opportunity to realize that your anxiety about your body was unfounded. Your ability to take part in and enjoy rewarding and gratifying experiences has very little to do with your weight.

In Sue's case, her body image had become distorted at a young age because of her history of obesity. No matter how thin she became, she never recovered to the point where she recognized her thinness. Any small increase in her weight made her feel that she was beginning a rapid weight-gain trajectory. Also, she was overly sensitive about issues of physical appearance as they related to her interactions with other people. Because of these issues, she relied too heavily on people to "keep her safe" from food and to "make her feel better about herself" by valuing her physical presence and appearance.

Summary

This chapter addressed the issue of body-image concerns, one of the most salient and entrenched features of various eating disorders. We examined the common types of body-image concerns with which bulimics struggle, including overvaluing body shape and weight in response to social and cultural pressures; having received—usually from a young age—critical messages about weight, shape, and/or physical appearance; channeling other concerns into a preoccupation with weight and shape; exaggerating fears of weight gain following small gains after normalizing the pattern of eating; and avoiding pleasurable activities because of one's body-shape and weight concerns. Strategies for working through each type of body-related concern were introduced. Review the material presented here before proceeding to the next chapter.

Homework

✎ Begin to note situations in which body-image concerns become prominent. Identify the nature of the concern, note the consequences of being concerned, and use an appropriate strategy for addressing the concern, such as challenging problem thoughts, engaging in an alternative activity, using problem solving, or "just doing it"—participating in the activity in spite of your worries about your body.

✎ Continue all aspects of the program (keeping Daily Food Records, working toward a regular eating pattern, and engaging in pleasurable alternative activities). Continue to weigh yourself once a week and record your weight in the comments column of your Daily Food Record.

Take some time to review the contents of this chapter and complete the following self-assessment. Answer by filling in the correct words or phrases, or by circling T (True) or F (False). Answers can be found in the Appendix.

1. Name three types of body-image concerns common in eating disorders.

    _____

    _____

    _____

    _____

2. How can you manage your fears regarding the effects of a normal eating pattern on your weight and shape?

    _____

    _____

    _____

    _____

3. There is one "attractive look" for women, including expectations for weight and shape, that is considered a universal standard.   T   F

Chapter 10   *Solving Problems*

Goals

- To identify problems that lead to binge eating

- To learn a method for solving these problems

Review of Previous Chapter

You should be continuing with all aspects of the program. Remember to complete your Daily Food Records and note all factors that contribute to any problematic eating episodes. Make an effort to eat more regularly and use pleasurable alternative activities to delay or prevent overeating episodes. You should also be weighing yourself weekly, noting your weight in the comments column of your Daily Food Record.

These behavioral strategies remain essential to the process of recovering from bulimia. You and your therapist should review your progress in maintaining these behavior strategies before proceeding to new topics.

Overview

This chapter will present a method to help you solve problem situations and dilemmas that can lead to binge eating. The information you obtained from your analysis of binge triggers should have helped orient you to the environmental, internal, and social factors that contribute the most to your binge-eating episodes. The method that will be described here will help you work through complex problems that involve multiple binge triggers, in a structured and organized fashion.

Sue's Problem Managing Evenings off from Work

Let's reconsider our patient Sue. During Phase 1 of treatment, she struggled to make gains in response to the initial recommendations for behavior change, although she did begin to consider the alternative perspectives (about food, eating, her body, and weight maintenance) offered to her in the program. Her eating patterns and foods were regularized to some extent, thus decreasing the frequency and size of her binge-and-purge episodes. Still, she had very ingrained notions about the importance of maintaining a certain type of body shape and a certain weight. She held extreme fears about the effects normal eating would have on her weight. She continued to experience strong cravings for sweets, particularly a certain type of chocolate cookies, which she did not allow herself to eat when she was not bingeing. Her binge episodes and other out-of-control experiences with her food, purging, mood, and self-perception also visibly and predictably worsened when Sue found herself alone. Thus, being alone was a high-risk situation for her that significantly increased her risk for binge eating. Sue's eating habits were normal when she spent several consecutive days with other people, but this awareness left her feeling rather helpless and dependent on others to "solve" the problem of her eating disorder.

Low Mood and Problem Thoughts

Why did Sue have trouble allowing herself to simply relax, or to undertake pleasurable activities when she was alone? Why did she instead resort to binge eating? She had not thought about this much before, but it seemed that the experience of being alone triggered a perception of feeling not only lonely but also unlovable and unattractive. The more Sue fell into a funk about her looks and state of loneliness, the more likely she was to turn to overeating and purging as a distraction. She learned inadvertently to rely too much on the behaviors of her eating disorder, which provided a partial and short-lived solution to her problems, a solution that in the long run made her feel only more depressed, unattractive, isolated, fat, and hopeless. Sue also acknowledged that because her life had revolved for so many years around the issues, challenges, and mere "logistics" associated with her eating disorder, she had lost sight of a number of pleasurable hobbies and activities that she had once enjoyed, either as a way to relax or to express her creative or masterful side. For Sue, it was the combination of emotions and thought patterns, an absence of interesting and pleasurable activities, and a limited number of social connections and supports that very predictably intensified her vulnerability to binge eating, particularly during evenings alone.

Continued Dietary Restriction

Despite having shown some mild response to Phase 1 of treatment, Sue maintained a fairly restrictive diet that allowed for "treats" and indulgences only in the context of a binge or if strongly suggested by others who were enjoying these foods. She attributed her restrictive eating patterns to concerns about losing control and fears of the subsequent weight gain she "knew" would happen once she began eating these foods regularly. Even though her weight was in the low–average range for her height and had not budged at all during the first several weeks of treatment, Sue was still adamant that she would start to gain weight consistently if she began to eat more normally. Sue understood intellectually that a restrictive eating style increased her risk for bingeing by contributing to her strong cravings for sweets and chocolate and her frequent sensations of hunger. But, in a more emotional and admittedly somewhat irrational way, she was too terrified about weight gain to systematically increase the number of regular meals and snacks she was eating or the amount of food consumed (that she was willing to keep down) at each meal. Over time, with strong encouragement from her therapist and her significant others, Sue became increasingly willing to incorporate a small amount of chocolate into her meal pattern. She would eat it as a snack or as a dessert to reduce her cravings. However, during the early stages of treatment, Sue was still too afraid of weight gain to do more than talk about her fears of making the changes recommended by this program.

Abstaining from Pleasurable Alternative Activities

Sue acknowledged that she had given up many hobbies and recreational activities when she suffered from bulimia. She found it difficult to fully engage in pleasurable activities much, partly because she usually felt anxious, upset, and exhausted. She also felt untalented and ashamed that she was no longer able to do things as well as she might have in the past (for example, tango dancing had been a recreational pursuit at certain points in her adult life). It was hard for Sue to decide what she wanted to do because she was frequently "too tired" to do much of anything. Also, she was afraid she would do whatever she chose to do "the wrong way." Therefore, even formerly enjoyable activities did not necessarily give her pleasure. When faced with a night alone, saddled with these troubling and self-critical thoughts, burdened by a low mood, and around a large stock of desirable binge food, Sue had a hard time believing that any activity, other than bingeing, would feel good.

Nevertheless, Sue began to acknowledge that bingeing was less gratifying and rewarding than it had once been. She found that she was unable to "just do it" in the unconscious way that she had before, given her awareness of her goal to overcome her eating problems. Thus, each time she decided to binge, she experienced much more inner turmoil than she had had before. This added to, rather than detracted from, the painful thoughts and feelings she was trying to avoid. She knew that developing tools for self-soothing, other than binge eating and purging, was necessary so that, at times of distress, she would be able to use them. She accepted that it would take practice using these alternative activities (and thinking more optimistically in order to feel more positively) so that she could use them easily and comfortably during periods when she was at high risk for bingeing.

Accumulation of Risk Factors

On any given night alone, in spite of her commitment to recover from bulimia, several factors—namely, a low mood, negative thoughts and feelings, the impression that there was nothing else to do that would feel as good, and the presence of attractive binge food—combined to increase Sue's risk for bingeing and purging. Her problem, while complex, could be summarized as follows: "I am alone tonight, without my boyfriend or my kids, and I feel tired and in a bad mood, and I just want to eat chocolate cookies, even though I am trying to overcome this problem with bulimia." Based on the problem description, Sue was in conflict. She was aware of the risk inherent in her situation (e.g., being alone at night) and feared that she might lapse into her usual pattern of binge eating if left to her own devices without better alternatives. However, she was also deeply committed to her recovery from bulimia. She needed a system of generating alternative strategies for handling her negative thoughts and feelings without resorting to binge eating.

Deficits in Problem Solving

Like Sue and many other bulimics, you may experience some difficulty trying to solve complicated problems that have often led you to binge in the past. One aspect of your problem-solving deficits might involve your difficulty defining the problem you are facing. You may have a tendency to describe problems in overly vague and general or too detailed or negative terms. Or, you may confuse yourself by including multiple problems in your description, making the issue(s) that you face seem overwhelming, overly complex, and unsolvable.

To move forward in defining your problem, you need to identify the core issue you are struggling with. Ask yourself, "What is really bothering me here?" or "What am I most upset about?" If you find that the problem you describe includes extremely global or negative terms such as, "I will never get over my eating disorder," you can use the challenging problem thoughts method (presented in the next chapter) to correct some of these thinking errors. Using this method will help you learn to see your problem(s) in a more balanced way. Other steps in the problem-solving method can be tricky to master. For example, Step 2 involves *brainstorming*. This means thinking through *all* the possible solutions to your problem, regardless of how silly or crazy they may seem. People who needlessly screen might prematurely rule out potentially viable alternatives. The remaining steps of the problem-solving method include evaluating alternative solutions, making a decision about which solutions to apply to your problem, and following through. When you are first learning how to use this method, it is especially helpful to practice it in writing. A blank form for your use is included here, but it can also be helpful to use the back of your Daily Food Record to work through problems by examining the context in which certain of your binge-eating episodes occur.

The Problem-Solving Method

Step 1: Identify the Problem

The aim here is to be as specific as possible when identifying your problem. Problems that are described in general, vague, or exaggerated terms are harder to solve, and so they make you feel ineffective when you try to solve them. If you find that your problem description includes "larger-than-life" issues, you probably need to redefine your problem. To increase the probability of successfully solving your problem, you need to define it specifically and accurately.

Sue's example: "I am alone tonight, and I'm tired and in a bad mood and believe, on some level, that the only way to deal with these feelings is to binge on chocolate cookies."

Step 2: Brainstorm Alternative Solutions

The goal of this step is to brainstorm all the possible solutions to your problem. Generate ideas without screening or evaluating. This requires that you think creatively about the various alternatives and also learn to value, appreciate, and uncritically accept your own ideas. The process of brainstorming will result in a comprehensive list of alternative solutions to any problem you face. It will enhance your sense of worth and control as you begin the process of overcoming your habitual, maladaptive strategies for resolving problems.

Note in Sue's example that she includes a range of solutions, some of which are more adaptive than others.

Sue's example:

1. Binge and purge on chocolate cookies to avoid having to deal with my feelings of loneliness, and satisfy my cravings for chocolate

2. Try to allow myself to eat some cookies without losing control

3. Go out to a restaurant and eat one portion of dessert there

4. Get out of the eating situation altogether—go for drive, go to the gym, etc.

5. Call a friend

6. Try to engage in a project like copying recipes from the paper or writing letters

7. Clean my apartment

Step 3: Evaluate Each Solution

After generating a number of solutions during the brainstorming step, begin to evaluate each one. At this stage, you should take each item on the list and consider how practical the solution is and how effective it could be. This step is extremely important. Whereas it is obvious that you would not want to choose a solution that is impractical or unlikely to be helpful, it is sometimes difficult to accurately appraise a potential solution without working through the steps of a formal evaluation. This step helps you fine-tune your search for the solution(s) that will provide the "best fit" and prove the most effective in solving the problem at hand.

Sue's example: Evaluating alternative solutions

1. Binge and purge on cookies to avoid dealing with feelings and satisfy cravings for chocolate cookies.

   Practicality: Can do it because cookies available at home. (+)

   Effectiveness: In short term, would satisfy cravings, make me full, finish up the food so it would be gone, and, hopefully, help me distance from and forget uncomfortable thoughts and feelings. *But,* on the negative side of the balance, a decision to binge would totally undermine my recovery effort. (−)

2. Try to allow myself to eat some cookies without losing control.

   Practicality: Easier said than done! I don't think I can even open up a box of cookies without losing control and bingeing. (−)

   Effectiveness: Won't be effective for the reasons cited above. (−)

3. Go to a restaurant and order and eat one portion of chocolate dessert there (knowing that I will keep it down)!

   Practicality: Many cafés are open at this hour, and I don't have a problem going out alone. (+)

   Effectiveness: This may work if I go to a place that offers desserts that I like and where I can also relax and feel comfortable. The only downside would be if I start to dwell on worries about the effects of the food on my body. Note: The method for challenging problem thoughts, presented in the next chapter, can be helpful in working through these types of worries—so adding in some cognitive-restructuring tools could enhance this potential solution. (+)

4. Get out of the situation (go for a drive, go to the gym, etc.).

   Practicality: Easy to drive somewhere in my car to delay immediate self-destructive behavior like bingeing. (+)

   Effectiveness: Would need to combine this with another strategy (like deciding to go to the gym or to have some chocolate dessert at a restaurant or to challenge some problem thoughts using the methods I can learn in the next chapter). Otherwise, my low mood and negative thoughts and feelings are unlikely to change, and since the box of chocolate cookies remains at home, I would still be at risk for eating too much of it— maybe the entire box. (+/−)

5. Call a friend.

   Practicality: I do have a few people that I could call, but they may not be home, in the mood to talk with me, or able to offer me support tonight. (+/−)

Effectiveness: If the conditions are right, this might be helpful, but it would be hard to know in advance if I could rely on contact with other people to make me feel better tonight. (+/−)

6. Try to engage in a project like copying recipes from the paper or writing letters.

    Practicality: Although I do have recipe and other letter-writing projects to complete, I'm not that interested in them and am too keyed up right now to focus on doing a good job with the writing; I would probably still be preoccupied with eating. (−)

    Effectiveness: Unlikely for this solution to work unless I address my problem thoughts and feelings first. I would need to combine this solution with something else (challenging problem thoughts, allowing myself to have a reasonable portion of something sweet to eat) for it to work. It seems like staying at home alone doing anything at all will increase my risk for bingeing. (−)

7. Clean my apartment.

    Practicality: I know that I should do this, but there is no way that I can force myself to clean right now. And, this is certainly not a *pleasurable* alternative activity, just an alternative! (−)

    Effectiveness: Trying to force myself to do something that I feel I *should* do *but don't want* to do when I am at risk for binge eating is only going to make things worse. It is hard for me to get motivated to clean my apartment, and if I start pushing myself to try to do it now it is likely that I will give up and binge. (−) Note: If you have already learned how to challenge problem thoughts (as discussed in the next chapter), and if problem thoughts are relevant to the situation at hand, you can apply this method as an additional alternative solution, separately or in conjunction with other solutions.

8. Challenge thoughts about "being a loser," and so on, using the cognitive-restructuring method described in the next section.

    Practicality: I can learn to use the method to challenge these types of distorted, negative thoughts about myself, such as, "I'm a loser for not having plans, etc." I just have to force myself to pick up a notepad to do it in writing so that it sticks. I think I'm motivated enough to be able to do that tonight. (+)

Effectiveness: Usually my mood improves when I challenge these types of thoughts. Tonight that would decrease my desire to binge and facilitate my ability to engage in alternative activities that are inconsistent with binge eating. (+)

Step 4: Choose a Solution

The objective here is to choose one solution or a combination of solutions based on your assessment and your intuition.

Sue's example: Based on Sue's assessment, the most feasible alternatives appear to be leaving the situation specifically to go to a café, where she can satisfy her craving for chocolate cookies by having a dessert served to her in one reasonably sized portion. After that, if need be, she can use methods to challenge any residual problem thoughts and/or use any simple self-soothing strategies (such as taking a hot bath or calling a friend) when she gets home, if she's still distressed. The other options were ruled out as impractical or ineffective. In addition, Sue added a component to her problem-solving strategy: In keeping with her commitment to refrain from binge eating and purging, she decided to limit her access to the box of chocolate cookies kept at home by leaving it in her storage locker before getting into her car for the drive to the café.

Step 5: Follow Through

The objective here is to follow through by implementing the solution(s) you chose.

Sue's example: Sue followed all the steps involved for each of the solutions she chose, and reported a good outcome (no binge eating or purging) in response.

Step 6: Reevaluate the Problem and Review the Problem-Solving Exercise

After implementing the solution, consider the extent to which you succeeded in solving the problem. If necessary, revisit the problem-solving procedure to fine-tune certain aspects of the process if any of the steps have proven more difficult than expected (e.g., problem definition, brainstorming). To fine-tune your use of the method, it is essential to practice it regularly, ideally several times each week.

Sue's example: Sue was able to apply the solutions she had generated during the exercise, and she had no difficulty using the formal problem-solving method in this particular situation. In the past, she had recognized a tendency to define problems too broadly and also to prematurely screen alternative solutions before fully thinking them through. She had improved in these areas by practicing the method in a variety of problem situations that had occurred over the course of treatment.

What If You Can't Follow Through with the Solution?

Some individuals have reported that their successful use of the method "on paper" does not translate into their ability to follow through with the intended solutions, even though they appear both practical and effective. If you find that you are unable or unwilling to implement the solutions you've generated through formal problem solving in a given situation, you need to talk to your therapist so that the two of you can explore the reasons for this and develop strategies for moving beyond it.

The worksheet on page 146 can be used for problem solving. You may photocopy the worksheet from the book or download multiple copies from the Treatments *ThatWork*™ Web site at www.oup.com/us/ttw.

Summary

This chapter presented a method for solving problems and dilemmas that can trigger binge-eating episodes. Effective problem solving includes accurately defining the problem, creatively brainstorming potential solutions, systematically evaluating the practicality and effectiveness of each solution, and astutely selecting and implementing one or a combination of the solutions you've generated. One type of solution involves challenging troubling thoughts that may play a role

Problem Solving Method Worksheet

Step 1: Identify the Problem

Be specific!

_____

_____

_____

Step 2: Brainstorm all Possible Solutions

1. _____
2. _____
3. _____
4. _____
5. _____
6. _____
7. _____
8. _____
9. _____
10. _____

Step 3: Evaluate the Practicality and Effectiveness of Each Solution

1. _____
2. _____
3. _____
4. _____
5. _____
6. _____
7. _____
8. _____
9. _____
10. _____

Step 4: Choose a Solution

_____

Step 5: Use the Solution

Step 6: Review the Outcome

_____

_____

in the problem situation. As stated above, instructions in this method for cognitive restructuring are presented in the next chapter. Finally, the chapter encouraged you to talk to your therapist if you have been unable to translate your "on-paper" solution into real action. A blank form for writing out the problem-solving method was included for your use. Review this chapter to make sure that you fully understand and can easily implement the method before beginning the next chapter.

Homework

✎ Continue all aspects of the program (keeping Daily Food Records, working toward a regular eating pattern, and engaging in pleasurable alternative activities). Continue to weigh yourself once a week and record your weight in the comments column of your Daily Food Record.

✎ Practice the problem-solving method (in writing) at least once this week.

Self-Assessment

Take some time to review the contents of this chapter and complete the following self-assessment. Answer by filling in the correct words or phrases. Answers can be found in the Appendix.

1. List the five steps involved in effective problem solving.

    _____

    _____

    _____

    _____

    _____

2. Note some of the errors one can make in attempting to complete the problem-solving exercise.

_____

_____

_____

_____

3. What should you do if you find that you have not been able to implement practical and effective solutions to your problem?

_____

_____

_____

_____

Chapter 11   *Challenging Problem Thoughts*

Goals

- To identify your negative, problem thoughts

- To learn to change these thoughts through cognitive restructuring

Review of Previous Chapter

We hope you have found the formal problem-solving method introduced in the last chapter to be useful when dealing with situations that trigger your binge eating. Don't forget to practice the problem-solving exercise a few times each week. Record your attempts, using the Problem-Solving worksheet. You should also be continuing with other aspects of the program. During the past week you should have made an attempt to consume a few of your least-feared foods in appropriate situations. You should also be recording your daily food intake and refining a regular pattern of eating that includes three meals and two snacks per day. You should note not only the contents and quantities of foods you ate but also the context in which you ate, to reveal potential binge triggers such as hunger and troubling thoughts, feelings, and interpersonal interactions. These factors may play a role in creating the types of problem situations you addressed in the last chapter. Before you begin this chapter, make sure you have reviewed the last chapter, understand it, and have been able to implement the recommended strategies.

Overview

This chapter will continue the discussion of salient problem thoughts as factors that contribute to your bulimic episodes. A review of the types of processing errors and repetitive problem themes that seem to dominate the thinking patterns of bulimics and others will be included. A method of cognitive restructuring that will help you identify, challenge, and replace these "hot" problem thoughts with more adaptive alternatives will be introduced. Your therapist will help you learn and rehearse this method during the next few sessions, and you will be encouraged to practice it on your own between sessions.

The Link Between Problem Thoughts and Behaviors

As discussed in Chapter 8, some of the factors that trigger binges originate in the social environment (such as interpersonal interactions), and some come from within you. The latter include hunger, thoughts, and feelings, or some combination of thoughts and feelings, sometimes referred to as "hot thoughts" or "hot cognitions." One of the most common triggers of binge eating is distorted thinking that may encompass a variety of issues, including specific worries about shape and weight, current conflicts in your life, or general concerns about situations in your life, your self-worth, your acceptability to others, and so on.

At this point, you might still be unaware of the types of specific thoughts or thinking patterns that lead to binge eating. You may feel that the whole process of bingeing is automatic and beyond your control. However, when you consider the range of possible binge triggers, your thoughts actually represent a type of trigger over which you have a fair amount of control. To identify the problem thoughts or "hot cognitions" that are the most significant contributors to your bingeing, focus on the very behavior you are trying to extinguish. Examine closely the situations that you have found to lead to binge eating. As you've learned, there are many factors that can disrupt your progress toward the goal of stopping your bingeing behavior. In many cases, problem thoughts are the reason that progress stalls. You can begin to challenge your negative thoughts by recalling the thought-related issues that contribute to your binges.

If you are surprised by the idea that your thoughts strongly influence your eating behavior, you are not alone. Like others with eating disorders, you may not have considered this idea until now. Partly, this may be a result of your "spacing out" before, during, and after a binge. As mentioned, this is a fairly typical experience. If you characterize your binges this way, it is likely that you have little sense of any of the thoughts and feelings that might have had an effect on your eating behavior. Once you become more aware of the link between your thoughts and your eating behavior, you can learn how to use this observation in many different ways. You can learn to interpret instances of feeling at risk for bingeing or times when you find yourself actually engaged in bingeing as a signal that you may be reacting to distorted interpretations or negative themes. Or, you might notice that you have some of these difficult thoughts running through your mind. Knowing that you are having troubling thoughts can help you identify the situation as high-risk, and you should take extra precautions by using your problem-solving tools and the methods to challenge problematic thoughts (these will be explained later in the chapter). Cognitions linked to your problematic eating episodes can be characterized as "hot" in the sense that they are presumed to be closely associated with the intense and/or negative emotions that trigger your episodes of problematic eating behavior. One of the tricky aspects of managing these "hot" problematic thoughts is that you may end up taking them much more seriously than you should. These thoughts appear to be realistic and, in your mind, may represent the absolute truth. The mix of these "hot" cognitions and the associated strong emotions makes it quite difficult, if not impossible, to come up with a more balanced and rational perspective.

Given this difficulty, the most helpful method for challenging these problem thoughts is to first notice their occurrence, either by recognizing a negative mood or the fact that you are in the act of bingeing and/or purging or by observing your own thought process and knowing that these thoughts are on your mind. Once you master this first step, you will need to capture the essence of the particular problem thought(s) and then apply a method to challenge the rationality of the thought. The rationale for engaging in this type of exercise is obvious. If some aspect of your thinking style plays a role in triggering your problem eating episodes, then altering your thinking patterns should help decrease the frequency of these episodes. By the time you completed Chapter 8, you should have compiled a preliminary list of the types of thoughts that tend to occur before your binge-eating episodes. In this chapter, we will help you examine these thoughts in more detail. You will be encouraged to take note of the two areas through which cognitive triggers can be identified and addressed: problem-thinking *processes,* which are the patterns of distorting or misinterpreting information, and persistent troubling *themes* that seem to occupy your attention.

Let's begin with a discussion of thought processes. A helpful analogy compares the way you think to a lens that either helpfully corrects or unhelpfully distorts your vision. In considering your thinking patterns, the lens represents the manner in which you interpret your experiences. As an individual with bulimia, you view your experiences through an "eating-disordered" lens. As a result, you magnify certain pieces of information (such as those pertaining to food, eating, weight, or shape) in a manner that is consistent with several types of interpretation errors. In general, these errors involve perceptions that can be overly rigid, extreme, selective, or negative. An example of a cognitive-processing error (selective attention) is represented by your selectively paying attention to (and likely judging) one aspect of a situation while discounting another. For example, you may focus on the fact that you ate one cookie during the week and disregard the fact that you ate very healthfully the rest of the week.

Let's return to Sue's therapy to provide an example of the way in which distorted thoughts and the related behaviors can be addressed in a therapy session by using the week's Daily Food Records.

T: It sounds like some of the rules you have, such as "I'm going out to dinner tonight, so I can't eat very much at all during the day," set you up to binge—and those are rules you will need to break down eventually.

S: That's pretty much it, I think. And then I'm starving by the time we get to the dinner. So that was Thursday, my birthday. All I had after breakfast were two chocolate chip cookies for the entire day until we went out to dinner.

T: That was your birthday. So you had a piece of dry toast and egg whites and one package of cookies because of your rule that "if I'm going out to dinner, I can't eat very much at all during the day." What was going on that day that might have kept you further stuck in that way of thinking, without trying to challenge your thoughts and behaviors more?

S: Because it was my birthday, I wanted to have the cookies during the day, and I knew that the double whammy of some cookies and a dinner out would be way too much. I felt guilty for wanting them but convinced that I *had* to have them at some point. And then I felt even worse knowing I would have the dinner later, and I definitely thought, "Well, tomorrow for sure will be a weight-gain day."

T: You felt guilty for wanting them and guilty for having them but knew you'd feel deprived if you didn't, all the while thinking, "I shouldn't be eating anything because of the dinner out later—I will definitely gain weight this way."

S: I felt guilty for wanting them. I should have been allowed to have a fun day and have whatever I wanted. Instead, it became, "Oh God! I ate these."

T: What would you do differently if you could do that day over again, if you could alter your thoughts and your eating habits? What ideally would you want to see happen on that day?

S: I would like to have enjoyed it—the whole day, the package of cookies, just two of them, and the dinner out. I would like to have had some healthier ideas about what was going on. That it was my birthday, that it would be OK to basically eat in moderation what I wanted to eat, cookies and dinner out, and that even if I did gain a couple of pounds—and maybe I wouldn't weigh myself the next day—it would be worth it because I would have enjoyed my day.

T: What you're saying is that you were in a high-risk situation in that you weren't able to conjure up the thoughts and behaviors that you identified above, that you really needed to work hard on your thoughts, and to work hard to use some problem solving to figure out how to handle the entire day because you were alone for most of it. That, ultimately, the goal of treating yourself well and having a special day and feeling safe and secure with all your decisions, including the ones you made with food, was what you were after.

This sample interaction from Sue's therapy session illustrates one of the ways in which an individual with an eating disorder may adopt a distorted perspective in evaluating his or her experience.

Sue selectively focused on the issue of "food rules" and on falling into eating a specific problem food (chocolate chip cookies) while failing to look at the bigger picture to understand what her options were, or to identify any aspects of the situation that she did take control over (e.g., not bingeing or purging). Selectively paying attention to only the negative aspects of a situation makes an individual more sensitive to other perceived deficits or flaws. This can lead to the kind of emotional upset that further contributes to binge eating.

Another type of thinking error typical of bulimic patients is drawing conclusions about weight-change trends based on their weight over just a week or two. For example, an individual who noticed a small gain of 1–2 lbs in a given week might fail to consider the many explanations for this small weight change, such as fluctuations in body fluids, an increase in the bulk and weight of food consumed and kept down, issues connected to the menstrual cycle, over-exercise, constipation, and so on. Any of these (or a birthday dinner out, as in Sue's case) might account for an insignificant weight gain of a few pounds that remains only a day or two, before normal eating patterns are resumed. An eating-disordered individual might instead jump to the conclusion that they had evidenced a *real, lasting, and possibly progressive* weight gain. It is very common for bulimics to jump to the conclusion that once they gain weight, regardless of whether it is actual weight gain or is caused by any of the factors just discussed, they will continue to do so. Another example, this one illustrating a specific type of problem thought about eating, is the mistaken perception that a given eating episode, because of the contents or the quantities consumed, has "ruined the entire day," will automatically lead to weight gain, and/or warrants a full-blown binge-and-purge episode. This type of reasoning represents some of the interpretive errors we describe later in the chapter.

Have you had the experience of thinking about situations in the ways just described, or in rigid, black-and-white extremes? Like other bulimics, you may be affected by distorted perceptions not only in the realm of your eating disorder but also with respect to general feelings and attitudes about yourself. You would not be alone if you struggle with concerns about self-worth, the need to be perfect, or the need to be accepted and approved of by everyone. You will explore these problem thoughts in therapy in an attempt to challenge and correct any errors in interpretations. At the same time, it is useful to discuss the origin of these beliefs and to learn strategies to refute the legitimacy of the source(s) that led to the development of these attitudes.

No matter what the type of distortion, a cognitive error usually results in an inappropriate or illogical conclusion about any given issue at hand that leads to negative feelings and some form of faulty coping behavior. For example, if you truly believe after one minor episode of overeating that you are a "failure" with respect to managing your eating and that your "whole day is shot," it makes sense that you might give up on that day altogether and decide to either restrict your food or binge-and-purge for the rest of the day. In this case, the "lens" through which you viewed your eating episode resulted in magnification of the meaning of one less-than-ideal eating episode. A more reasonable and balanced perspective that would not have led to negative feelings or unhealthy eating might have involved the following interpretation: "I ate more than I wanted, so I will not eat as much at my next meal."

Types of Interpretive Errors

1. All-or-nothing, dichotomous reasoning: Seeing things in absolute, black-and- white categories, for example, good–bad, right–wrong, and so on.

    Examples:

    "Either I am dieting and doing well, or I am overeating and doing terribly."

    "Unless I come in every week with no binge episodes, I'm a total treatment failure."

    "Once I eat any bad food, like anything sweet or with fat in it, the whole day is shot."

2. Overgeneralization: Using one negative event to color your perception of a series of events that may or may not be related.

Examples:

"I gained 2 lbs during the second week of treatment, so I know I will keep gaining 2 lbs every week."

"One time I binged on potato chips, so I can never again consider eating them."

"When I was a teenager, people teased me about my weight; so, if I put on any weight now, I will be teased again."

3. Magnification of negatives, minimization of positives: Blowing negative events out of proportion while dismissing positive events.

Examples:

Refer to Sue's dialogue with her therapist presented earlier.

"Even if I didn't binge in that one situation, I *felt* like doing it, so it's still a failure situation."

4. Catastrophizing: Overestimating the negative consequences of events.

Examples:

"If I gain 5 lbs, everyone will notice."

"Others will notice my weight gain, and I won't be able to stand that, so I can't make plans to see anyone."

"I had a bad week with eating, so I think I should just quit the program."

5. Selective abstraction: Basing a conclusion on isolated details, while ignoring contradictory and more salient evidence.

Examples:

"No one talked to me at the party, so it must be because they see me as fat and ugly."

"If I lost 10 lbs, especially below the waist, then my whole life would be different."

"I tried one feared food during the week, and I gained a pound. I'm sure that's the reason, so I have to go back to eating all carbohydrates and no fats."

Identifying and Revising Problem Thoughts

In order to change unhelpful patterns of thinking, you must first notice that a problem thought has occurred. Strong feelings, the occurrence of the behavior you want to change (binge eating or purging), or both, are signals indicating the presence of a problem thought. The next step is to figure out the *essence* of the *underlying* problem thought. Sometimes several related problem thoughts, when grouped together, support one core belief that if challenged could correct an entire group of associated thoughts. In attempting to identify the core problem thought from an initial thought or idea, ask yourself about the meaning of the thought: "If that was true, then what?" Do this until you think you've reached the underlying concern. You will know when you've identified the core problem thought because you will have a realization such as, "That's it!" When you have this "Aha!" or "Eureka!" feeling, you know you've identified the essence of your real concerns. For example, if you push yourself to understand the meaning of the problem thought "I feel fat," you might get in touch with the fact that "feeling fat" means not being liked, being rejected, and not having a romantic partner. The final realization you have about your problem thought is often the core or "hot" cognition" that you will be able to work with most effectively. At the same time, it is useful to challenge other important thoughts that may not represent the core issue but that may be problematic in their own right. For example, it would be valuable to gather evidence to support or refute the thought that you are fat, even if this thought is linked to other underlying issues.

Remember, the first step to challenging your problem thought is to recognize that a problem thought has occurred. The most useful cues are strong feeling states and/or the occurrence of the behavior you want to change (binge eating or purging). Eventually, you may become such a good self-observer that you are able to signal yourself when these thoughts enter your mind. You can help yourself along in the process of becoming aware of your problem thoughts by noting them in the comments column of your Daily Food Record. Once you identify at least one problem thought, you can take the next step, which involves challenging the thought by gathering up *objective* evidence to support and cast doubt on it. The method to challenge problem thoughts consists of four steps. A fifth step links your revision of the initial problem thought to following through with an adaptive behavior.

Method for Challenging Problem Thoughts

Step 1: Identify the underlying problem thought.

Step 2: Gather objective evidence or data to support the view behind this thought.

Step 3: Gather objective evidence to argue against this view.

Step 4: Based on the supporting and opposing evidence, come up with a reasoned conclusion that counters the original problem view.

Step 5: Link this exercise back to your behavior by determining a course of action based on your logical conclusion.

When using this cognitive-restructuring method, keep several points in mind. First, this strategy is most useful when applied to core underlying problem thoughts. A core thought or belief likely crops up in many different situations, so if you challenge and correct it and revise your behavior accordingly, you will be able to realize change in a variety of situations. Second, cognitive restructuring relies on your use of *objective* rather than subjective evidence. Subjective evidence includes your feelings, which can be distorted just like your thoughts can. Any time you support an argument for or against an underlying problem thought by saying, "Because that's how I feel," you are relying on your subjective judgment, which may not reflect reality. Gathering objective evidence for or against the problem thought requires that you consider a reasoned and logical perspective. This may be difficult for you because it requires that you expand your perspective to consider information you usually ignore and disregard. Your therapist can be very helpful in providing an alternative, objective perspective and input that will help strengthen your ability to eventually view situations in a more balanced light. Finally, once you gather objective information that can help you revise the problem thought, your goal should be to formulate an alternative thought that will "stick" as a permanent revision that can be called forth in related situations and used to direct you to more-adaptive behavior.

Here is another example from Sue's therapy:

T: Let's talk about weight and weighing in. You said your weight is 138, and you're 5′9″.

S: At least that's what they told me here.

T: We use this kind of measure called "BMI" or "body mass index" to think about weight. Basically, it calculates weight for your height. It's just a big range that one can consider as "normal" or "average" for a certain height. That's how it's used. You're 5′9″, and you weigh 138 or so. Your BMI is right there in the normal range. We normally consider "normal" to be a BMI between 18 and 25 or 26. You're about between 20 and 21. And you're right there in the lower end of average, and the only point in bringing that up is that there's a lot of room to roam back and forth in that range. We really encourage people to think in terms of a weight range rather than a set number, so that's why I'm just bringing up the construct of BMI. It's just another way to be thinking about weight, but we won't refer to it much here in the treatment. More importantly, though, we need to address two things. First is expectations for weight changes while you're in treatment, and then developing a healthy pattern of weighing. Now you've been a person who's weighed yourself a lot, and you said that yesterday you weighed yourself 10 times.

S: Every time I ate I weighed.

T: What did you find when you weighed after eating?

S: You know what I found? I didn't gain weight like I gained before.

T: So, that almost shows you, too, that the scale isn't that sensitive because having eaten 24 ozs of cookies, you should have gained 24 ozs. About a pound and a half or so.

S: Well, I threw it all up.

T: You threw it all up. When you do that, are you thinking that weight changes as registered by the scale in those instances would reflect an actual change in your lean body mass or your fat weight?

S: Well, I weighed myself this morning, and I weighed myself once today, and it was after that cantaloupe. I didn't eat much of that cantaloupe, but I was up 2 lbs. And I'm trying to not panic. I really, really tried. But I just kind of got off and thought no, it couldn't possibly be.

T: What would it mean if you gained 2 lbs after eating the cantaloupe? What could that possibly mean?

S: I don't know.

T: All it means to me is that the cantaloupe weighs 2 lbs, right? What else could it mean?

S: It means that I gained 2 lbs. That means that there are 2 lbs of something more on me. And it'll be right in the hips. That's the other thing I know.

T: Is there any part of you that sees your interpretation as a little bit off? What I'm saying is, if you eat a 2-lb cantaloupe, you're going to weigh 2 more pounds as registered by the scale, whereas you're saying, "Well, no, it means that I'm gaining weight in my hips and I'm 2 lbs bigger."

S: That's where the 2 lbs will go and, yes, I think that even though it's supposed to have 200 calories in it, it's the weight and not the calories, so it still comes up 2 lbs. And it'll be 2 lbs tomorrow. It's the number.

T: So the number on the scale is really, really important to you.

S: Yes, even if the logic is there to explain things another way, that doesn't suggest real weight gain. I still rely on the numbers, and they still make me feel good or bad.

T: Well, clearly, this is something we will have to work on over time in the treatment. First, reducing the frequency of your weigh-ins, so that you don't react to arbitrary changes in the numbers on the scale, and second, challenging the types of extreme and problematic thoughts that come up for you in response to seeing your weight. It really has been demoralizing for you to use the scale in this way, and we will have to stop it, as hard as that may sound!

S: Well, it sounds impossible, although what I am doing makes me feel terrible, too.

The Challenging Problem Thoughts worksheet on page 162 can be used for challenging and correcting core problem thoughts. You may photocopy the worksheet from the book or download multiple copies from the Treatments *ThatWork*™ Web site at www.oup.com/us/ttw.

Summary

This chapter presented a rationale for learning to identify and challenge problematic thought processes. These thoughts might involve troubling themes, distorted interpretations, or specific irrational thoughts or cognitions. These problem thoughts are typically triggers for binge-eating episodes, so it is important to learn how to identify, challenge, and modify them. You may become aware of the presence of a problem thought because you are thinking about bingeing and/or purging or because you are already engaged in these behaviors. Also, you may notice that you are feeling intense, negative emotions. Examples of types of interpretive errors, such as all-or-nothing thinking and magnifying negatives and minimizing positives, and problematic themes were presented. Finally, a method for identifying and challenging these problem thoughts was introduced. The method includes learning to link the problem cognitions, strong feelings, and maladaptive behaviors, and then gathering evidence to support or refute the offending thoughts in the hope that any asso-

Challenging Problem Thoughts Worksheet

Step 1: Identify the Underlying Problem Thought

Step 2: Evidence to Support

Step 3: Evidence to Refute

Step 4: Reasoned Conclusion Based on Columns of Evidence

ciated feelings and related behaviors can be modified. Sample dialogues between Sue and her therapist were included to illustrate the process of using these techniques. After completing the chapter, you should review it to make sure you understand and are able to implement the recommended strategies before proceeding to the next chapter.

Homework

✎ Continue all aspects of the program (keeping Daily Food Records, working toward a regular pattern of eating, and engaging in pleasurable alternative activities). Continue to weigh yourself once a week and record your weight in the comments column of your Daily Food Record.

✎ Use the Challenging Problem Thoughts worksheet to practice the cognitive-restructuring method on at least one occasion to challenge and correct any core problem thoughts you notice.

Self-Assessment

Take some time to review the contents of this chapter and complete the following self-assessment. Answer by filling in the correct words or phrases. Answers can be found in the Appendix.

1. Describe each of the steps of the exercise to challenge problem thoughts.

    _____

    _____

    _____

    _____

2. Name some of the types of cognitive errors that can lead to faulty interpretations or conclusions.

_____

_____

_____

_____

3. How can you identify a "hot" cognition or thought?

_____

_____

_____

_____

Chapter 12

Understanding More About Interpersonal and Emotional Triggers

Goals

- To identify your emotional binge triggers
- To learn strategies to help you manage high-risk situations

Review of Previous Chapter

Remember to complete your Daily Food Records and note all factors that contribute to any problematic eating episodes. Make an effort to eat more regularly and use pleasurable alternative activities to delay or prevent overeating episodes. You should also be weighing yourself weekly, noting your weight in the comments column of your Daily Food Record. The last chapter addressed body-image concerns, and you should be attempting to make changes in your thoughts and behaviors consistent with improving your body image. Make sure you review and understand the material presented in the last chapter before proceeding to the next.

Overview

In this chapter, we discuss the types of emotions and interpersonal-relationship experiences that can trigger binges. The chapter introduces methods that will help you become aware of signals that may indicate you are at risk for binge eating because of emotional or interpersonal stressors, and describes strategies that can help you manage these high-risk times.

In Chapter 8, we introduced the concept of binge triggers, categorizing triggers as external, social, or internal. Since completing that chapter, you should have been regularly noting your most significant binge triggers in the comments column of your Daily Food Record.

What types of triggers appear to be most prominent in precipitating your binge episodes? Based on our experience working with bulimics and binge eaters, we would expect that a large proportion of these triggers involve negative mood states that sometimes occur in conjunction with difficult interpersonal interactions. Take a moment now to review the material on mood and social triggers that you completed in Chapter 8. You will have an opportunity to update your lists of mood and interpersonal triggers in the space provided below. Then review your recent Daily Food Records to reflect on the contextual factors that have been predominant in contributing to your binge episodes. This chapter will help you focus on and examine emotional and interpersonal binge triggers in more depth.

Low Moods, Interpersonal Interactions, and Bingeing

How are feeling states, interpersonal interactions, and binge eating related? Bulimic patients frequently report that a negative mood is the most frequent trigger to binge eating. Negative moods are often caused by problems with interpersonal interactions. It is helpful to review the entries you've made in the comments columns of your Daily Food Records to find instances where your mood was low or depressed. Examine these instances in detail and look for places where your negative mood may have been related to an interpersonal problem or issue. Like others with eating disorders, you may have a tendency to personalize and blame yourself when you are feeling low, when in fact your mood may be linked to a social transaction that you initially overlooked or dismissed as unimportant.

Research suggests that negative moods, even those that don't last very long, have several effects. First, moods such as depression, anxiety, loneliness, or anger appear to drive an actual loss of control over eating in addition to causing a series of related, self-recriminating cognitions, such as "I'm such a loser—no wonder no one likes me," "I have no willpower," or "I am a pig." Second, when you are in a negative mood, you may perceive your food intake, and your body shape and weight, differently. There is a greater likelihood that you will classify an eating episode as a binge, regardless of the amount of food eaten, and that you will view your body shape and weight as excessive or unacceptable. It is also likely that being in a bad mood may lead you to overestimate the amount of food you have eaten, making you feel like giving up, for example, "I've already blown it, so why not have some more?" Even if these perceptions (that you are fat, that you overate, etc.) are heavily influenced by a negative mood, they still feel "real" and contribute to the binge-eating cycle of dieting, bingeing, and purging. Finally, many individuals with eating disorders feel that binge eating offers them an escape from their negative feelings (even if short-lived). There is evidence that negative feelings do decrease during the binge-and-purge episode, but then they worsen after the episode is over.

Which feelings or moods are most closely related to your binge episodes? Use the space provided to describe the mood factors that were instrumental in triggering recent binge-eating episodes. Also, briefly describe the role of this feeling in triggering your binge. Did you binge to feel better? Or to escape or numb yourself from the feeling? Or do you binge in response to having inappropriately labeled a prior eating episode as excessive, for example, because you were feeling bad?

Mood Triggers: _____

_____

_____

_____

For many individuals with eating disorders, interpersonal relationships are very important and provide a great deal of gratification. However, they can be frustrating and upsetting as well. Many individuals with eating disorders are "people pleasers," devoted to trying to make others happy, sometimes at their own expense. More than anything, they want to be liked. For this reason, eating-disordered patients may have difficulty getting into disagreements or conflicts. It may also be especially hard for them to receive criticism or negative feedback of any type. Never easy for anyone, the mildest interpersonal slight can traumatize individuals with eating disorders. On the other hand, many with eating disorders also crave and need space at times and may not be skilled at asking for it directly. The types of interpersonal stresses that can lead to problematic eating episodes are listed here.

- Having disagreements, conflicts, or arguments

- Receiving negative feedback or criticism

- Finding out that someone is not pleased with you or doesn't like you

- Sensing that someone intended to hurt you, or intends to hurt you in the future

- Needing space and feeling "crowded" by friends or loved ones

That is just a partial list of the types of interpersonal triggers, some of which may apply to you. It is important for you to create a list of your own. Think through the interpersonal-relationship factors that seem to be most closely linked to your recent binge-eating episodes. You may use your Daily Food Records to jog your memory about the nature of the interpersonal issues most closely linked to your binges. You will want to pay attention to who you were with, the nature of the particular interaction, the general quality or character of your relationship with the person, what might have been going on in the relationship or in the specific instance, and how you were thinking and feeling at the time. You might then want to distill those interpersonal elements down to their essence so that you can create your list based on these brief descriptions. It is important to also briefly note your ideas about how the interpersonal interaction affected your eating.

Interpersonal-Relationship Triggers: _____

_____

_____

_____

_____

Now that you've increased your awareness of the link among your mood states, interpersonal interactions, and binge-eating behaviors, you can begin to learn strategies for decreasing the likelihood that these interactions and feelings will lead to a binge or other problem behaviors. First, you will learn to signal or cue yourself that you are experiencing a strong mood state that increases your risk for bingeing, or that you have, or are currently engaging in, an interpersonal interaction that is likely to upset you. To learn how to do this, you will have to observe yourself regularly and consistently. This shouldn't be hard because you've been keeping regular food records for quite some time now. Once you've determined that you are experiencing a negative mood state, you have acknowledged that you're at risk for bingeing, and you need to figure out a strategy to manage this risk. It may be beneficial to repeat the word "mood" to yourself as a reminder of the risk and the perspective-altering effects of your mood (e.g., when in a funk, you tend to see things much more negatively than they really are). It is important to identify the particulars of your mood or feeling state so that you will be able to pinpoint its origin. Is the mood based on self-criticism, a physiological lull stemming from hunger or exhaustion, or a conflict-laden interpersonal interaction? If it is caused by conflict, exactly what type of problematic interaction is it? Once you have identified the mood and its origin, you can take steps to work through the mood state constructively, that is, *without acting on it in a manner that is self-defeating, such as by binge eating or purging.* Instead, your goal is to develop some plan of action along the lines of the problem-solving method introduced in Chapter 10.

For example, an individual who realizes she has fallen into a funk because she is tired and hungry might take note of this fact and then attempt to solve it by applying each and every step of the problem-solving method. She would note that she was hungry and tired and at risk for bingeing and then strive to come up with appropriate solutions that might include sleeping, eating, and/or engaging in a pleasant alternative activity incompatible with eating that would enable her to modulate her feelings without engaging in a self-destructive behavior like bingeing. The following steps may help as you attempt to better manage the strong feelings that contribute to bingeing. Use the space provided to practice this method.

Managing Mood States

1. Acknowledge that your general mood or feeling state has increased your risk for bingeing. Use the cue of "mood" to remind yourself of your altered perspective and the need to take precautions.

2. Identify the particular mood or feeling state.

3. Attempt to pinpoint its origin: Is your mood state based on physiological factors (being hungry or tired), specific thoughts (about performance or worth), or an interpersonal conflict?

4. Based on the source that you identified in step 3 above, develop a plan of action for managing the mood or feeling state without acting on it in a manner that is self-destructive. For example, use problem solving (including engaging in alternative pleasurable activities) or challenge the problem thoughts to delay or prevent bingeing.

The process of managing the interpersonal contributions to low mood states and binge eating is similar. First, develop a framework for understanding that interpersonal interactions can contribute to binge eating in various ways. In certain situations, the link between a social interchange and binge eating might be straightforward and obvious. For example, you might have an argument with a friend and then feel a strong urge to binge. In other situations, you may need to do a bit more detective work to identify the interpersonal underpinnings of a desire to binge. Negative feelings or self-reproaching thoughts resulting from a relationship issue may predominate and take you "off track" with respect to identifying and working on the relationship problem. Again, the low mood state itself (or an urge to binge) can be used as a signal that you need to ask yourself about the possibility that a relationship problem is involved. If so, you should cue yourself about your high risk for bingeing by using the word "relationship." Next, you should work to develop some understanding of the nature of the relationship issue that is troubling you. You may be responding to an acute situation, for example, becoming upset

Managing Mood States

1. Acknowledge that your general mood or feeling state has increased your risk for bingeing. Cue yourself with the word "mood" as a reminder of your altered perspective and need to take precautions.

2. Identify the particular mood or feeling state.

_____

_____

_____

_____

_____

_____

3. Attempt to pinpoint the origin of the mood or feeling state.

_____

_____

_____

_____

_____

_____

4. Develop a plan of action for managing the mood or feeling state without acting on it in a manner that is self-destructive. Do one or more of the following:

   • Complete a problem solving form.

   • List alternative pleasurable activities.

   • Complete a Cognitive-Restructuring worksheet.

because your boyfriend did not call when you were expecting to go out to dinner with him, and then bingeing as a result of both hunger and other feelings (e.g., disappointment, rejection, anger). On the other hand, the relationship issues contributing to your binges may be more general and less closely linked in time to a given binge episode. For instance, you may be in a marriage in which your expectations about the level of closeness and intimacy have not been met. More chronically, you may binge eat out of frustration and loneliness. While both of these interpersonal scenarios can certainly trigger binge episodes, different strategies are required for working to resolve them. In the first instance, where your boyfriend didn't call you, you might apply the problem-solving method to examine the problem at hand: that you are hungry and upset because your boyfriend did not follow through with the dinner plans you made. Part of the method to solve your problem might involve challenging problematic thoughts to correct a tendency to distort or over-personalize the situation. For example, you may be inclined to jump to the conclusion that your boyfriend wants to end the relationship, when in fact you enjoyed considerable time together over the past few days and he informed you then that the dinner plan was tentative, depending on what was happening at his job. An additional solution would involve making a decision to eat, possibly going out on your own, preparing and eating a meal at home, or going out with a girlfriend. Finally, you would want to identify alternative methods to cope with the feelings of anger and depression caused by your boyfriend's behavior. These might include engaging in some enjoyable activity, such as going to a movie, exercising, or taking a hot bath.

With respect to the more general, longer-term interpersonal issues, a plan of action might involve using the strategies above to make your life more immediately satisfying, and then identifying your expectations for the relationship and small steps that you can take toward achieving or reevaluating your expectations. Your therapist can be extremely helpful in working with you to understand the influence of long-standing interpersonal issues on binge eating and to carve out a reasonable set of strategies that you can use to improve the relationship, including revising your expectations. In general, themes of communication, apologizing, forgiving, seeking apology, taking responsibility, attributing responsibility, and airing a problem rather than pushing it aside might be helpful, in general, as you think about the interpersonal issues connected to your eating disorder. Use the space provided to practice this method.

Managing Relationship Problems

1. Notice that a relationship problem has increased your risk for bingeing. Cue yourself using the word "relationship."

2. Attempt to clarify the nature of the issue and its effect on your mood. (Who is involved? What is the conflict about? Is it acute or long-standing?)

3. Work on resolving the problem. First, take steps to manage your mood (see the above exercise on managing mood states). Then address the immediate relationship problem at hand, using problem solving or the problem-thoughts exercise.

4. If long-term relationship issues are involved, talk with your therapist about a strategy for working through these issues.

What If I've Already Binged or Feel I Can't Do the Exercises?

Some patients are convinced that it is not worthwhile to retrospectively view the factors that led up to a binge. This is absolutely untrue. Even after you've binged, it is worthwhile to gather data that will ultimately increase your awareness of the role of factors like moods and relationship issues that have contributed to your decision to binge. After the fact, you need to work backward from the binge to the thoughts and feelings that surrounded the decision to binge, and then attempt to identify the predominant feeling state that initiated the chain of events. This method can be extremely valuable in adding to your understanding of your eating disorder while you are still recovering and before you have been able to regularly delay binges long enough to work through the recommended methods.

Some patients may feel like they "can't" use these methods because their feelings are too strong to allay without a binge. They feel that it takes too much effort to concentrate, decide to delay bingeing, shift their focus to active coping rather than passive resignation, and

Managing Relationship Problems

1. Acknowledge that a relationship problem has increased your risk for bingeing. Cue yourself using the word "relationship."

2. Attempt to clarify the nature of the issue and its effect on your mood.

_____

_____

_____

_____

_____

_____

_____

_____

_____

_____

_____

_____

_____

_____

_____

3. Work on resolving the problem. Manage your mood.

4. If long-term relationship issues are involved, talk with your therapist about a strategy for working through these issues.

work through the methods described. We hope you can learn to use signals and cues to stay focused on your short- and long-term objectives (overcoming binge eating), even in the midst of an overpowering, negative mood state. Based on our experience with eating-disordered individuals, we believe you can learn to tolerate very strong feeling states. Working to master overcoming the tendency to binge under duress will provide you with an opportunity to apply the exercises described here and gain a fresh perspective on your feelings and your options for modulating them. It might help to carry around a simple reminder, such as a small notebook and pen, as a cue that you have decided to work on learning to tolerate and manage your feelings by following the steps above.

Summary

This chapter provided a discussion of two common binge precipitants: negative mood states and interpersonal conflicts. We advised you to use the comments column in the Daily Food Record to increase your awareness of these triggering factors. In addition, we recommended a method for learning to manage problem moods and relationships. This method involves drawing the link between the mood or relationship issue and a heightened risk for bingeing; acknowledging a high risk state; identifying the specific cause; using methods to challenge problem thoughts or work through problem situations to resolve the immediate cause; and using therapy to understand and take steps to resolve longer term relationship issues. Although some patients say they "can't do" the method or that it is not useful to do it after they've binged, our experience suggests otherwise. We believe that most people can complete the exercise by relying on a self-generated cue to delay giving in to a low mood state; we suggest carrying around a pen and pad of paper. Also, the method can be extremely useful, even after the fact, to retrospectively examine obstacles to coping with factors that continue to trigger binge episodes.

Homework

✎ Continue all aspects of the program (keeping Daily Food Records, working toward a regular eating pattern, and engaging in pleasurable alternative activities). Continue to weigh yourself once a week and record your weight in the comments column of your Daily Food Record.

✎ Use the mood and/or relationship-management methods on at least one occasion before your next session.

Self-Assessment

Take some time to review the contents of this chapter and complete the following self-assessment. Answer by filling in the correct words or phrases. Answers can be found in the Appendix.

1. What are the two most common precipitants to binge episodes?

   _____

   _____

   _____

   _____

2. Name the steps included in the method to manage mood states.

   _____

   _____

   _____

   _____

Chapter 13

Maintaining Changes After Treatment

Goals

- To consider methods of maintaining your progress

- To create a relapse-prevention plan

Review of Previous Chapter

You have now been presented with all the interventions of the cognitive-behavioral treatment program for bulimia and binge-eating disorder. Phase 1 of the program focused on teaching you how to alter your eating-disordered behaviors. Phase 2 taught you how to identify high-risk situations, problem thoughts, and negative feelings. By making it to the end of treatment, you have clearly demonstrated a significant response to the program. If you continue to apply the strategies you have learned, you will maintain the progress you've made.

Overview

This chapter will discuss the ending of treatment and will present strategies for maintaining the gains you've made after treatment is over. You will be assigned the task of creating a written relapse-prevention plan that lists all the interventions that have been helpful to you. This plan will help you "get back on track," should you experience a worsening of any aspect of your eating problem. You will also be encouraged to consider a "lapse not relapse" mind-set that will put mild setbacks into perspective.

Beyond providing a relatively short-term therapeutic experience, the goal of this treatment program is to facilitate your ability to learn behavior-change strategies you can continue to use on your own, long after therapy is over. Regardless of the extent to which you achieved your treatment goals, the tools introduced here should enable you to maintain and expand upon these changes on your own. You may indeed feel that some of the changes you've made thus far have become second nature, such that you feel confident that you can continue these without the benefit of ongoing participation in this program. On the other hand, there may be those of you who still feel somewhat shaky about the extent to which you've really overcome your eating problems, and you may wonder about the possibility of experiencing a setback after ending treatment. This chapter will present a strategy for maintaining and expanding upon your treatment gains.

Treatment may conclude differently for individual patients. Some of you will continue to work with your therapist, using alternative methods to address various issues. Perhaps you and your therapist will agree that discussion of the eating disorders issues and CBT "booster" sessions will occur only as needed. For others, ending therapy may mean ending the therapist–patient relationship. Remember, though, you may be able to make arrangements with your therapist to meet periodically if necessary. Although this type of ending may feel more permanent, the development of a relapse-prevention plan is important for everyone completing this program, whether you are continuing in other therapy or not.

How do you end therapy? First, it is essential that you summarize all the work you have done in treatment. You should focus both on the progress you've made and on the areas that still need improvement. To begin this process, you might want to revisit the outcomes summarized midway through treatment (see Chapter 6). Compare your progress then to now and also consider the changes you've made with respect to incorporating feared foods and understanding your binge triggers, problem thoughts and situations, and body-image concerns. (For your convenience, the Summary of Progress sheet on page 179 includes the list of therapy outcomes examined at mid-treatment; we have added to the list those issues that were addressed during the sec-

Summary of Progress: Mid-Treatment to Completion

Phase 1 Skills

Number meals per week mid-treatment _____

Number of meals currently _____

Number snacks per week mid-treatment _____

Number of snacks currently _____

Number of days *at least* 3 meals, 2 snacks mid-treatment _____

Number of days *at least* 3 meals, 2 snacks at completion _____

Number of days exactly 3 meals, 2 snacks mid-treatment _____

Number of days exactly 3 meals, 2 snacks at completion _____

Improvement in days eating 3 meals, 2 snacks _____

Number of weeks weighed one time _____

    Mid-treatment _____

    At completion _____

Mid-treatment use of alternative activities _____

Use of alternative activities at completion _____

    1————————2————————3————————4————————5
      much worse   no change   much better

Rating of mastery in managing eating situations (1–5)

    Mid-treatment _____

    At completion _____

Phase 2 Skills

Number of feared foods incorporated each week mid-treatment _____

Number of feared foods incorporated each week at completion _____

    1————————2————————3————————4————————5
      much worse   no change   much better

Ability to challenge problem thoughts (1–5) _____

Ability to work through problem situations (1–5) _____

Improvement in body-image concerns (1–5) _____

If overweight:

Number of days per week exercised

    Mid-treatment _____

    At completion _____

    1————————2————————3————————4————————5
      much worse   no change   much better

Reduction in fat intake (1–5)

    Mid-treatment _____

    At completion _____

    1————————2————————3————————4————————5
      much worse   no change   much better

ond half of treatment.) We hope the second half of treatment added a level of depth to the behavioral changes you made in the first part of the program, increasing your ability to maintain these changes over time and across a variety of situations.

After summarizing your progress, it is important to identify the areas that still need work. Based on your review of the therapy outcomes, which problem areas warrant ongoing attention? For example, it would not be uncommon for someone to complete the program, reduce binge eating and vomiting to almost no episodes per week, be able to identify triggering problematic thoughts and feelings, and still struggle to a great degree with body-image concerns that could potentially result in the dietary restriction that triggers bingeing. In order to anticipate potential problem areas, it is important to identify current problems and take whatever steps are needed to minimize their influence on your behavior. Your feelings about leaving therapy are important. These may range from relief at having "graduated" from a structured program, to sadness and loss associated with leaving a supportive environment and therapy relationship. Give yourself an opportunity to reflect on these feelings and accept them as a normal part of moving on. Consider your completion of therapy an important transition in your life, with inherent gains and losses. You might want to take some time to write your feelings down. Finally, if you are completing the program and ending the work with your current therapist, what are your options? We discourage those who complete the program from immediately getting involved in any other form of psychotherapy. Alternative methods for understanding and treating the same problem can sometimes confuse matters. Share your thoughts about additional therapy with your therapist. He or she will have a comprehensive understanding of your options.

Developing a Maintenance Plan

The objective here is to help you create a relapse-prevention or maintenance plan that you can use to get yourself back on track if you experience a setback with your eating disorder. A *setback* or *lapse* is any eating situation that you feel is less than the "flexible ideal" that you typically strive for. That might mean anything from overeating at a breakfast buffet when you're not even hungry to engaging in a binge-and-purge episode following a stressful dinner with relatives. A set-back involves a *brief* (e.g., a few episodes, hours, or days) return to a problem behavior that seemed resolved. What distinguishes a set-back or lapse from a *relapse* is that a relapse represents a return to the problematic behavior *for an extended period of time.* You might be inclined to think of an exacerbation as a relapse if you begin to experience the same out-of-control, helpless feelings you had before your participation in this program. It may be helpful to remember, however, that eating disorders can "flare up" in times of stress. Therefore, it is best to prepare yourself for foreseeable stressors by using the methods presented in the program (e.g., making sure that your eating is regular and satisfying, that you work through problematic thoughts related to the upcoming situation, that you identify alternative methods for handling the situation, and last, but not least, that you consider the possibility that a lapse might occur and for that reason you make a commitment to getting back on track as soon as possible). You should also be considering the types of situations that might throw you for a loop and trigger a binge. Having oriented you to these terms, the next step is for you to develop maintenance or relapse-prevention plans that will help you stay in control of your eating to the extent possible and facilitate your getting back on track as quickly and easily as you can if you experience a lapse.

The elements that should be included in your plan for maintenance are those aspects of the treatment that were most helpful, a summary of the progress you've made in treatment, and where you're at with respect to your recovery at the end of therapy. Finally, your plan should also address potential problems, such as an anticipated family reunion that might trigger former desires to binge, and so on. For example, many patients continue to consume three meals and two snacks per day, including a variety of formerly feared foods. They also find it beneficial to record their food intake in detail using Daily Food Records, to weigh themselves weekly, and to become aware of potential binge triggers, like problem situations and thoughts, and consistently challenge and work through these. After identifying the helpful ingredients of your treatment program, you may choose to write them out in a narrative fashion. For example, "If I begin to feel that I am having problems controlling my intake, I will, first, start keeping food records, and then I will organize my eating into three meals and two snacks per day," and so on. Alternatively, you may want to simply list the strategies that were useful, putting them in order of usefulness. In terms of summarizing their progress and anticipating future problem areas, most patients jot down a few notes about their status, especially the measurable outcomes (e.g., frequency of binge eating and purging) and what additional improvements they would like to make. Again, some comments about anticipated stressors are important and can productively generate future-oriented problem solving. Remember, it is essential that you keep your maintenance plan close at hand! A lost maintenance plan is no help to anyone. A sample completed maintenance plan and a space for you to create your own are included.

Remember Sue? She completed her treatment program having made some significant progress overcoming her binge-eating and purging behaviors. However, she still had negative thoughts about her body shape and weight, despite having maintained a weight that was below the normal range for her height throughout the entire program. For Sue, resuming strict dieting was a risk factor (for resuming the binge-purge cycle) that might be triggered by disappointment about "numbers on the scale" that were higher than expected, feelings of fullness, "bloatedness," "thickness," or "fatness," and/or "looking heavy," or in any other way feeling badly about her body. Sue was aware of these ongoing vulnerabilities and acknowledged the value of maintaining aspects of the program to limit the potentially adverse effects of her negative body image. See Sue's maintenance plan shown in Figure 13.1.

We hope that the experience of participating in this program was valuable and productive. It is our expectation that by consistently applying the strategies learned here, you can continue to enjoy better control and mastery over your eating and related concerns.

What worked for me in the program was eating three meals and two or three snacks each day. I never experienced the level of hunger that had previously set me up to binge eat. Plus, I let myself eat some of the foods, like cookies, that I craved—foods that I had feared before. So the cravings never got out of control. Although I have always been critical about my body weight and shape, at least with the once-weekly weigh in I was able to reassure myself that my weight was not continually increasing in response to eating more food and keeping it down. It also got me out of the habit of weighing every time I ate anything or went to the bathroom — a habit that was demoralizing and led to even more confusion about my weight. I think it would be helpful to stay with the one-time a week weigh in.

But I'm worried that even having had the experience of learning to eat more normally and not really gaining weight, I will persist in wanting to lose weight (in fact I can honestly admit right now that I do want to lose weight despite the fact that I know that my weight is in the "normal" range). It is particularly hard for me when I think I've had too many cookies or other sweets in addition to my meals, and it's especially hard to deal with feeling fat when I'm alone. At those times, I'm tempted to purge, binge and purge, or lapse into restriction mode again. What I need to do at those high risk times is challenge some of the problem thoughts that come up having to do with the "fat" feelings and the longer term consequences of starting the eating disordered behavior again. Also, it might be helpful to use the problem solving exercise to come up with strategies for dealing with those uncomfortable feelings that don't involve reverting back to the eating disorder. (I've noticed that when I'm having a hard time it has always been helpful to make a commitment to eating the next regularly scheduled meal or snack.) Therapy has helped a lot and probably participating in some type of group or more counseling would be good for me at some point if I need it.

Finally, I need to continue to challenge my views about the importance of looking a certain way. That people, my boyfriend, my kids, even in other social situations, don't judge me as harshly as I judge myself. I still struggle with the feeling of wanting to have a different kind of body in certain ways, but I know that I can choose to tune in to these kinds of thoughts to a greater or lesser degree if I want. And it is more consistent with staying on top of my eating disorder to push my body concerns to the back of my mind rather than keeping them alive in the foreground.

Figure 13.1 Sue's Relapse Prevention and Maintenance Plan

My Relapse Prevention and Maintenance Plan

Homework

✎ Create a relapse-prevention and maintenance plan.

✎ Remember to include a summary of your progress in treatment and thoughts about planning for any anticipated difficulties.

Self-Assessment

Take some time to review the contents of this chapter and complete the following self-assessment. Answer by filling in the correct words or phrases. Answers can be found in the Appendix.

1. What is the purpose of, and what are the elements included in, a relapse-prevention or maintenance plan?

    _____

    _____

    _____

    _____

2. Distinguish between a lapse and a relapse.

    _____

    _____

    _____

    _____

Appendix

Self-Assessment Answers

Chapter 1

1. An exaggerated sense of the importance of shape and weight; binge eating (rapid consumption of food when not even hungry and to the point of feeling uncomfortably full) or periods of binge eating alternating with food restriction; in Bulimia Nervosa, purging of food through vomiting, use of laxatives, or compulsive exercise; sense of self-esteem based on perceptions of shape and weight; maintenance of average or above-average weight.

2. **True.** Binges can be large or small, because the definition of a "binge" is highly subjective and seems to be based primarily on the perception that the eating was out of control. Depending on how the individual views eating (with a tendency for the more seriously affected individuals to experience almost any eating as a binge), eating episodes as small as 100 calories can be described as a binge. Data based on objective binge episodes—those large binges that have been classically considered the hallmark of bulimia—indicate that the average binge for an individual with bulimia consists of about 1500 calories and for the person with binge-eating disorder about 1000 calories and can range upward to 7000 calories.

3. Family history (biogenetic and environmental factors), sociocultural influences on women to be thin, low self-esteem, history of being teased for overweight condition.

4. Mixed feelings about starting treatment, lack of motivation, fear of change, involvement in other psychological treatment, other emotional problems that need treatment.

5. Bulimia Nervosa includes some form of purging; binge-eating disorder does not.

6. **False.** This program is also appropriate for the treatment of binge-eating disorder. Where necessary, special sections are included to address issues unique to binge-eating disorder. The differences in the treatment approach will be discussed by your therapist. Otherwise, the same general information and interventions apply.

7. Research studies have identified cognitive-behavioral therapy as an effective treatment that can lead to a total "cure" rate of about 65%. You can expect a very good outcome from treatment if you are able to make it a top priority in your life, if you are motivated to change enough to follow through on treatment recommendations, and if you have perseverance enough to persist in your efforts to get better, even when the going gets tough.

Chapter 2

1. The three phases are Behavior Change, Identifying Binge Triggers, and Relapse Prevention. The Behavior Change phase includes use of food records, prescription of a regular meal pattern of three meals and two snacks per day eaten at specific times, once-weekly weighing, and use of alternative activities. The Identifying Triggers phase includes introduction of "feared" foods, identifying risk factors that contribute to binge episodes, challenging problem thoughts, problem solving, and addressing body-image concerns. The Relapse Prevention and Maintenance phase includes reviewing progress made in treatment, developing a written relapse prevention and maintenance plan that lists the helpful strategies learned during treatment, addressing remaining problem areas and anticipating future problems, and devising a strategy for getting back on track following any setbacks.

2. Advantages of using a workbook: (a) structure and sequencing of treatment procedures and sessions; (b) can be used to prepare for sessions in advance; (c) can be used to review content of discussion after sessions; (d) can be used to educate signifi-

cant others; (e) following completion of treatment, serves as useful reference and "refresher" workbook.

3. Sessions include brief overview of progress since last session using food records as reference, detailed examination of food records, agenda for introduction of new topics based on record review, formulation of homework assignments, summary and wrap-up.

Chapter 3

1. Self-monitoring of the behaviors that, prior to treatment, were targeted for change.

2. Self-monitoring heightens your awareness of problem eating episodes and helps you understand the patterns, the surrounding contexts, and the specific factors that contribute positively or negatively to your problem. Use of food records can actually interrupt problem eating patterns by increasing your sense of accountability ("I don't want to do it if I have to write it down") or by helping you delay. Completed records can be a useful reminder about your progress over a number of hours, a day, or in the longer term. Because individuals with eating disorders tend to criticize themselves, data recorded in food logs can correct these types of perceptual errors so that you are more inclined to stay on track rather than respond to an unfounded belief that you've "blown it." Food records can also be used as a preventive tool to plan and record meals and snacks in advance.

3. The Daily Food Record is most helpful when entries are made as close to the time of eating as possible. The log can also be used to plan meals and snacks in advance.

4. Time of eating, food and liquid consumed (type and general quantity), place of eating, notations about whether or not the eating episode was considered a meal ({}) or binge (*B*), a notation to indicate whether purging took place (either vomiting [*V*], laxatives [*L*], or diuretics [*D*]), information about the

context of eating (including thoughts, feelings, interpersonal interactions), and weight (from once-weekly weighing).

5. Natural weight refers to the weight range in which your body will stabilize when you are treating it well—not restricting, bingeing, purging, or over-exercising.

6. Typically, individuals with eating disorders tend either to avoid or be compulsive about checking their weight—either never weighing, or weighing far too frequently. Once-weekly weighing is recommended so that you can obtain regular but not excessive feedback about your weight while you are making actual changes in your eating behaviors. Establishing a regular weekly weighing time that you follow with a structured activity can help desensitize you to the impact of "seeing the numbers" and also provide you a realistic perspective for understanding arbitrary fluctuations in weight (which everyone experiences) that may be due to fluid retention, the amount of bulk in the foods eaten, or variations in your monthly cycle.

7. **True.** Weight fluctuations are common and are due to a variety of factors including the amount of food and sodium consumed during the few days prior to the weighing, the amount of exercise, where someone is in her monthly cycle, etc. Individuals with eating disorders tend to exaggerate the meaning of these normal, minor fluctuations and interpret any shift upward as evidence of an uncontrollable trend of weight gain.

Chapter 4

1. Dietary restriction or purging, hunger, loss of control, binge eating, low self-esteem, weight and shape concerns. The model explains how dieting (stemming from shape/weight concerns and/or low self-esteem) results in hunger or deprivation, which leads to out-of-control binge eating, which may result in further restriction or purging, leading to lowered self-esteem and an increase in worries about weight and shape. The model illustrates a truly vicious cycle.

2. Although it may not seem to make sense to most individuals with eating disorders, the first step involves eating more, in order to eliminate the deprivation effects of dietary restriction.

3. Limiting the amount of calories taken in overall; decreasing or eliminating certain foods or food groups (such as cookies, ice cream, fats, sugars); reducing the number of eating episodes per day (skipping meals); relying on a series of extensive rules about what, when, and how much you should or shouldn't eat.

4. No. The results of many treatment studies based on this model suggest that most clients gain an average of 0 to 2 or 3 pounds while in treatment. Eating more and eating more regularly can actually help prevent weight gain by preventing the large binges, in which substantial numbers of calories were ingested (and not all could be purged). A regular pattern of eating, along with paying attention to food contents (specifically decreasing fat intake) and increasing exercise can be a useful strategy for weight loss (for individuals who are overweight) or weight maintenance for all others concerned about weight.

5. Pleasurable alternatives to binge eating can help delay or prevent binge eating altogether by elevating mood and decreasing boredom, allowing for an opportunity to rethink the pros and cons of bingeing, and to reconsider perceptions of the amount eaten or feelings of fullness when these might lead to a binge or purge episode.

Chapter 5

1. Dental and periodontal problems (including erosion of dental enamel and infections), swelling of the salivary glands, low potassium that may lead to cardiac arrhythmia, sensitivity to cold, dryness and coarsening of the skin, hair loss. When bulimia is associated with low weight, osteoporosis may occur, occasionally leading to bone fractures. Rare complications include vomiting blood from tearing in the esophagus and stomach rupture. Foreign objects may be swallowed during the course of a binge.

2. Binge-eating disorder tends to result in steady weight gain, so the medical complications associated with this disorder are the same as those associated with overweight and obesity. Among the conditions frequently seen are high blood pressure, diabetes, and increased levels of fat in the blood. Other complications include osteoarthritis, gall bladder disease, and menstrual disturbances. Individuals may also experience low self-esteem from the guilt and social stigma of being overweight.

3. There seems to be no advantage to stretching out the withdrawal time. No matter the pace, discontinuing laxatives is painful. Thus the "cold turkey" method is recommended. This can be made more comfortable by discussing in advance the expected physical side effects (bloating, cramps, temporary weight gain from fluid retention, and temporary constipation).

Chapter 6

1. Reduction in frequency of binge and purge episodes (absolute and percentage change); implementation of a regular eating pattern of three meals and two snacks; maintenance of once-weekly weighing; engaging in alternative activities instead of binge eating; sense of increased mastery and control over eating; if overweight, establishment of a regular exercise regimen; if overweight, decreasing fat intake.

2. **True.**

3. Individuals with eating disorders seem to interpret information through a lens colored by perfectionism, self-criticism, magnified negatives and minimized positives, and all-or-nothing extremes.

4. The most important thing you can do is to discuss your concerns with your therapist. He or she will help you evaluate your treatment response as objectively as possible, and if necessary, discuss other options that could potentially include addition of a medication or switching gears to another form of therapy.

Chapter 7

1. **True.** One form of restriction is avoidance of certain foods or food groups. Often, the foods on the "feared" or "avoided" list are foods that you like and crave—the very foods that you end up bingeing on.

2. The rationale for including feared foods in your meal plan is based on the model for understanding bulimia, as illustrated in the preceding answer. Essentially, the more you limit your access to satisfying foods, the more these foods will be desired and craved and—when hunger and other triggering factors reach a certain level—binged on. Regular use of feared foods interrupts this form of restriction, prevents or limits the sense of deprivation that accompanies restrictive dieting, and thereby can help decrease the frequency and size of binge-eating episodes.

3. Feared foods should be consumed at a time when you are not at high risk to binge (that is, in absence of risk factors such as extreme hunger or emotional upset), when you have limited access to the food in question (for example, a slice of cake at a restaurant, not a whole cake at home), when the situation is controlled (may include presence of others, no access to purging, or limited amount of time). It is important to experience a sense of mastery over feared foods by introducing them slowly and with caution in situations that meet the above conditions.

4. **False.** Avoiding certain foods or food groups, especially those that you like, can contribute to a sense of feeling deprived. Deprivation leads to loss of control when you are confronted with the avoided food, especially if you are hungry or otherwise at risk for overeating.

Chapter 8

1. Factors originating inside of you that may contribute to your binges are hunger, mood states or feelings, and thought patterns.

2. There are several strategies that you can use to minimize the effects of risk factors. The first is to keep up with the regular pattern of eating. If you are not hungry, your risk for bingeing

is substantially decreased. Secondly, you can engage in pleasant, alternative activities that can take your mind off the desire to binge as well as the other factors that made you feel like binge-ing in the first place. Chapters 10 and 11 will discuss other strategies for minimizing your risk for bingeing, including challenging problem thoughts and problem solving.

3. Many individuals with eating disorders attribute their binges to one type of internal factor, such as "lack of willpower," "personal weakness," "being in a bad mood," or "low self-esteem." They may fail to take into account other internal factors (such as hunger or certain thought patterns) and dismiss altogether the role of environmental factors such as interpersonal relationship issues.

4. The internal factor of hunger.

Chapter 9

1. Worries about the effects of normal eating on weight or shape; overvaluation of maintaining a low weight and slim body shape; longstanding beliefs about being fat, learned from messages given by other people; avoidance of pleasurable activities due to shape and weight concerns.

2. Consider the model for understanding binge eating, which states that normal eating offsets the big binges that contribute the most calories. If you have gained some weight, ask yourself how important it really is that you have gained the weight, and engage in behaviors that minimize its importance (for example, throw out old clothes that are too small). Also examine the pros and cons of weight gain versus staying bulimic. Hopefully, the costs of your bulimia will outweigh the costs of mild weight gain. Finally, tailor your meal plan (without restrictive dieting) and exercise regimen to facilitate a gradual loss of weight into a more healthy range.

3. **False.** Based on historical and cross-cultural data on preferences for women's (and men's) appearance, there is no one standard to define what characteristics are considered attractive. The current standards in contemporary Westernized societies, which

seem to prefer slimmer shapes in women, are certainly arbitrary because they have changed time and again over the years.

Chapter 10

1. Steps in effective problem solving: (a) Identify the problem—define as specifically as possible, in your own words. (b) Brainstorm about alternative ways to solve the problem. No screening here—get all of your ideas down on paper! (c) Evaluate the practicality and effectiveness of each potential solution. (d) Based on your evaluation and your intuition, choose one or a combination of solutions that you think will work best. (e) Use your solution(s) to solve the problem. (f) Evaluate the entire problem-solving exercise to determine if you need to work on improving any one step (for example, more ideas during brainstorming, more specific problem definition).

2. Overly vague, broad, detailed, or negative problem description; screening prematurely during brainstorming; failure to follow through with chosen solutions.

3. Discuss this dilemma with your therapist so that the two of you can explore the issues that may be blocking your continued progress.

Chapter 11

1. Steps to challenge problem thoughts: (a) Identify problem thought. (b) Gather objective evidence to support. (c) Gather evidence to dispute or cast doubt on. (d) Based on the evidence, come to a reasoned conclusion that counters the original problem thought. (e) Act accordingly.

2. All-or-nothing reasoning (seeing things in absolute, black-and-white categories); overgeneralization (using one negative event to color your perception of a series that may or may not be related); magnifying negatives, minimizing positives (blowing negative events out of proportion while dismissing positive events); catastrophizing (overestimating the negative consequences of events); selective abstraction (basing a conclusion

on isolated details while ignoring contradictory and more relevant evidence).

3. A "hot" cognition or thought is one that is associated with strong or negative feelings and a problem behavior, such as binge eating. You can get in touch with the "hot" cognition by identifying the first problem thought and asking yourself, "What are the implications if that is true?" or "What is the meaning of that?" You will know when you've identified the core of "hot" cognition by having an "Aha!" or "that's it!" reaction. The method for challenging problem thoughts works best when applied to a very salient or "hot" cognition.

Chapter 12

1. Low mood state and unsatisfactory interpersonal interactions.

2. Steps to manage mood states: (a) Note that you are in a low mood state and at risk for bingeing. Use the word *mood* as a reminder that you need to take precautions to prevent a binge. (b) Identify the particular mood or feeling state. (c) Attempt to pinpoint the origin of your low mood state: Is it based on physiological factors (being hungry or tired), specific thoughts (about performance or worth), or an interpersonal conflict? (d) Based on what you found in *c* above, develop a plan of action for managing the mood or feeling state without acting on it in a self-destructive manner. For example, do a problem-solving form (including alternative pleasurable activities) or challenge problem thoughts to delay or prevent bingeing.

Chapter 13

1. The maintenance plan is a tool that you can use to help you maintain and build upon changes you made during treatment. It includes a listing of the strategies learned in treatment that were most helpful and general plans for using these techniques should eating problems arise. Additionally, the plan should include a summary statement about the progress you made in treatment with respect to your expectations and about anticipated stressors or problem areas.

2. A lapse is a brief setback or return to a problem behavior (such as binge eating) that had been resolved. It differs from a relapse in that it is a short-term resurfacing of the problem in reaction to an identifiable set of circumstances or challenges. Any lapse can be viewed as an opportunity for learning more about the factors that continue to trigger binge episodes. A relapse, on the other hand, is a return to the problem behavior for an extended period of time.

About the Authors

Robin F. Apple received her PhD from the University of California–Los Angeles in 1991 and has published articles and chapters in the area of eating disorders. She has also cowritten a patient manual and a therapist guide that use cognitive-behavioral therapy to help patients prepare for weight-loss surgery. In her current role as associate clinical professor, Department of Psychiatry and Behavioral Sciences, Stanford University, she has an active role training postdoctoral psychology fellows and psychiatry residents to use CBT and other treatment techniques, and has provided short- and long-term individual therapy and group therapy for those dealing with eating disorders and a range of other issues. Dr. Apple also maintains a varied caseload in her private practice in Palo Alto, California, and she is a consultant with the county medical center's eating-disorders program, a contributor to a multi-center weight-loss surgery research study, and has been an expert witness in forensics related to weight-loss surgery.

W. Stewart Agras earned his medical degree from University College, London, England, in 1955 and then completed his residency and fellowship at McGill University, Montreal, Canada. He was an early leader in the field of behavior therapy. At the University of Vermont, he became interested in phobia as a model for psychotherapy research, and, in collaboration with Harold Leitenberg, PhD, discovered that exposure to the feared situation was a principal ingredient of treatment for phobias. After moving to the University of Mississippi Medical Center as chairman of the Department of Psychiatry in 1969, he established the department as an active research center focused on behavioral psychotherapy, establishing the psychology residency program with David Barlow. In 1973, he moved to Stanford University as a professor of psychiatry, establishing one of the first behavioral-medicine programs in the country, and becoming the first and founding president of the Society for Behavioral Medicine. When the upsurge in patients with bulimia nervosa occurred in the late '70s, he began research into the etiology and treatment of the disorder, conducting a number of important treatment trials for bulimia nervosa, together with the first treatment studies for binge-eating disorder. In addition, he has been president of the Association for the Advancement of Behavior Therapy and editor of the *Journal of Applied Behavior Analysis and the Annals of Behavioral Medicine,* and has twice been a fellow at the Center for Advanced Studies in the Behavioral Sciences.